The Complete Diabetic Mediterranean Diet Cookbook for Beginners

2000+ Days of Easy, Healthy Recipes for Diabetes & Prediabetes Beginners

Shaddey Zontgomery

Table of Contents

INTRODUCTION

Evolution of Mediterranean Diet

The Mediterranean diet has a rich and fascinating history that spans thousands of years. Its evolution can be traced back to the ancient civilizations that thrived in the Mediterranean region, such as the Greeks and the Romans. The diet has since undergone various changes and adaptations, but its core principles have remained consistent, making it one of the most celebrated and scientifically supported dietary patterns.

Ancient Origins:

The foundations of the Mediterranean diet can be found in the eating habits of ancient civilizations. These societies relied heavily on the bountiful resources of the Mediterranean Sea and the surrounding land. Their diets were primarily plant-based, incorporating a wide variety of fruits, vegetables, whole grains, legumes, and nuts. Olive oil, a key component of the Mediterranean diet, was a staple in their culinary practices.

The Influence of Ancel Keys:

The modern recognition and popularization of the Mediterranean diet can be attributed to the work of an American scientist named Ancel Keys. In the 1950s, Keys conducted the landmark Seven Countries Study, which examined the dietary patterns and health outcomes of different populations. His research revealed that individuals living in Mediterranean countries, such as Greece and Italy, had lower rates of heart disease compared to those in other regions.

Key Principles and Components:

The Mediterranean diet is characterized by several key principles and Key

principles and components:

- Abundance of Plant Foods: The diet emphasizes the consumption of fruits, vegetables, whole grains, legumes, nuts, and seeds. These plant-based foods provide a wide range of essential nutrients, antioxidants, and fiber.

- Healthy Fats: Olive oil is the primary source of fat in the Mediterranean diet. It is rich in monounsaturated fats, which have been associated with numerous health benefits, including reduced inflammation and improved heart health.

- Moderate Consumption of Fish and Poultry: The Mediterranean diet encourages moderate consumption of fish, particularly fatty fish like salmon, which are rich in omega-3 fatty acids. Poultry is also included in moderation.

- Limited Red Meat and Sweets: Red meat consumption is limited in the Mediterranean diet, and sweets and sugary beverages are kept to a minimum. Instead, the diet favors lean sources of protein and encourages natural sweeteners like honey or fresh fruits.

- Herbs and Spices: Mediterranean cuisine is renowned for its use of herbs and spices to enhance flavor. Commonly used herbs and spices include oregano, basil, rosemary, thyme, garlic, and cinnamon.

Scientific Support and Health Benefits:

Over the years, numerous studies have supported the health benefits of the Mediterranean diet. Research has shown that following this dietary pattern is associated with a reduced risk of various chronic diseases, including heart

disease, type 2 diabetes, certain cancers, and cognitive decline. The diet's emphasis on whole, unprocessed foods, healthy fats, and plant-based ingredients is believed to contribute to these positive outcomes.

Evolution and Adaptations:

While the core principles of the Mediterranean diet have remained consistent, regional variations and adaptations have emerged over time. Different countries and cultures within the Mediterranean region have added their own unique flavors and ingredients to the diet. For example, Greek cuisine incorporates more yogurt and feta cheese, while Italian cuisine features pasta and tomatoes.

In recent years, the Mediterranean diet has also been adapted to meet specific dietary needs, such as the Diabetic Mediterranean Diet. This variation focuses on controlling blood sugar levels by emphasizing low-glycemic index foods, portion control, and regular physical activity. It combines the principles of the Mediterranean diet with the specific dietary considerations of individuals with diabetes.

In conclusion, the Mediterranean diet has evolved over centuries, drawing inspiration from ancient civilizations and scientific research. Its emphasis on plant-based foods, healthy fats, and moderate consumption of animal products has made it a highly regarded dietary pattern worldwide. With its proven health benefits and adaptability, the Mediterranean diet continues to be a popular choice for individuals seeking a balanced and nutritious approach to eating.

What is Diabetics and its food list?

Diabetes is a chronic condition characterized by high blood sugar levels. It occurs when the body either doesn't produce enough insulin (a hormone that regulates blood sugar) or doesn't effectively use the insulin it produces. Managing diabetes involves maintaining stable blood sugar levels through a combination of medication, physical activity, and dietary choices.

For individuals with diabetes, following a balanced and nutritious diet is crucial. The Diabetic Mediterranean Diet combines the principles of the Mediterranean diet with specific considerations for managing blood sugar levels. It focuses on consuming whole, unprocessed foods that are low in added sugars and refined carbohydrates while emphasizing healthy fats, lean proteins, and high-fiber carbohydrates.

Here is a food list that aligns with the Diabetic Mediterranean Diet:

Fruits and Vegetables:

- Berries (strawberries, blueberries, raspberries)
- Citrus fruits (oranges, lemons, grapefruits)
- Apples
- Pears
- Leafy greens (spinach, kale, Swiss chard)
- Tomatoes
- Bell peppers

- Broccoli
- Cauliflower
- Eggplant

Whole Grains:

- Whole wheat bread
- Whole grain pasta
- Brown rice
- Quinoa
- Bulgur
- Barley
- Oats

Legumes:

- Lentils
- Chickpeas
- Black beans
- Kidney beans
- Pinto beans

Lean Proteins:

- Skinless chicken breast

- Turkey breast
- Fish (salmon, trout, tuna)
- Shellfish (shrimp, lobster, crab)
- Tofu
- Greek yogurt (low-fat or non-fat)
- **Eggs**

Healthy Fats:

- Extra virgin olive oil
- Avocado
- Nuts (almonds, walnuts, pistachios)
- Seeds (flaxseeds, chia seeds)
- Olives

Dairy and Dairy Alternatives:

- Low-fat or non-fat milk
- Low-fat or non-fat yogurt (unsweetened)
- Cheese (in moderation)

Herbs, Spices, and Flavorings:

- Garlic
- Onion

- Herbs (oregano, basil, rosemary, thyme)

- Spices (cinnamon, turmeric, cumin)

- Lemon juice

- Vinegar (balsamic, red wine)

Beverages:

- Water

- Herbal tea (unsweetened)

- Coffee (in moderation)

It's important to note that portion control plays a significant role in managing blood sugar levels. Monitoring carbohydrate intake and spreading it throughout the day can help prevent spikes in blood sugar. Consulting with a registered dietitian or healthcare professional can provide personalized guidance on carbohydrate counting and meal planning.

In addition to the food list, individuals with diabetes should limit or avoid foods that can cause significant blood sugar spikes, such as:

- Refined carbohydrates (white bread, white rice, sugary cereals)

- Sugary beverages (sodas, fruit juices, energy drinks)

- Processed snacks and sweets (cookies, cakes, chips)

- High-fat dairy products (whole milk, full-fat cheese)

- Fried foods

- Processed meats (sausages, hot dogs, bacon)

It's worth noting that individual dietary needs may vary depending on factors such as age, weight, activity level, and specific diabetes management goals. Working with a healthcare professional or registered dietitian can help create a personalized meal plan that suits individual needs and preferences while effectively managing blood sugar levels.

In summary, the Mediterranean diet is ideal for people with diabetes because it is rich in fiber, healthy fats, antioxidants, and whole foods. It can help to improve insulin sensitivity, prevent blood sugar spikes and crashes, reduce inflammation, and maintain a healthy weight. However, it's important to note that everyone's nutritional needs are different and it's always best to consult with a healthcare professional before making any significant changes to your diet.

Why the Mediterranean Diet is Ideal for Diabetics?

The Mediterranean diet is a healthy eating pattern that is rich in fruits, vegetables, whole grains, legumes, and healthy fats such as olive oil and nuts. It is also low in red meat, processed foods, and added sugars. This diet has been shown to be beneficial for people with diabetes for several reasons.

Firstly, the Mediterranean diet is rich in fiber which helps to slow down the absorption of sugar into the bloodstream. This can help to prevent blood sugar spikes and crashes which are common in people with diabetes.

Secondly, the Mediterranean diet is rich in healthy fats such as olive oil and nuts which have been shown to improve insulin sensitivity. This means that the body is

better able to use insulin to regulate blood sugar levels.

Thirdly, the Mediterranean diet is rich in antioxidants which help to reduce inflammation in the body. Inflammation is a key driver of many chronic diseases including diabetes. By reducing inflammation, the Mediterranean diet can help to improve insulin sensitivity and reduce the risk of complications associated with diabetes.

Finally, the Mediterranean diet is rich in whole foods which are nutrient-dense and low in calories. This can help people with diabetes to maintain a healthy weight which is important for managing blood sugar levels.

Foods to Embrace and Avoid

According to the Centers for Disease Control and Prevention (CDC), a Mediterranean-style diet can be beneficial for people with diabetes. This diet emphasizes eating plenty of fruits, vegetables, whole grains, beans, and nuts. It also recommends using extra virgin olive oil instead of butter or other oils. Dairy products and red meat should be limited, while sweets, added sugars, sodium (salt), and highly processed foods should be avoided.

The Mayo Clinic suggests avoiding saturated fats found in high-fat dairy products and animal proteins such as butter, beef, hot dogs, sausage, and bacon. Coconut and palm kernel oils should also be limited. Trans fats found in processed snacks, baked goods, shortening, and stick margarines should be avoided as well.

The Diabetic Mediterranean Diet focuses on making healthy and sustainable dietary choices that support overall health and blood sugar management. By incorporating a variety of nutrient-dense foods and practicing portion control, individuals with diabetes can enjoy a flavorful and satisfying eating plan that promotes stable blood sugar levels and overall well-being.

In general, people with diabetes benefit from eating higher fiber foods because these types of foods are metabolized slower and increase blood sugars at a slower rate. Whole grains and legumes also provide a large amount of carbohydrates; therefore, people with diabetes will need to be mindful of portions.

It's important to note that there is no one-size-fits-all approach to eating healthy. A diabetes care and education specialist can help create a diabetes meal plan that works for you.

Diabetic diets is bland while Mediterranean diet is full of flavors, how can the two work?

While it is true that some traditional diabetic diets may have been perceived as bland or restrictive in the past, the Diabetic Mediterranean Diet offers a flavorful and diverse approach to managing diabetes. By combining the principles of the Mediterranean diet with specific considerations for blood sugar control, individuals can enjoy a wide range of delicious and satisfying meals while still maintaining stable blood sugar levels.

Here's how the Diabetic Mediterranean Diet incorporates flavors and works effectively for individuals with diabetes:

- Emphasis on Whole, Unprocessed Foods: The Diabetic Mediterranean Diet encourages the consumption of whole and minimally processed foods, which are

inherently flavorful. Fresh fruits, vegetables, herbs, and spices are key components of the diet, adding a variety of tastes, aromas, and textures to meals. These ingredients can be used creatively to enhance the flavors of dishes without relying on added sugars or unhealthy fats.

- Healthy Fats for Flavor: The Mediterranean diet's use of healthy fats, such as extra virgin olive oil, avocados, nuts, and seeds, adds richness and depth to meals. These fats not only contribute to the overall flavor but also provide satiety and help regulate blood sugar levels. Healthy fats can be used in dressings, marinades, and sautés to enhance the taste of vegetables, proteins, and whole grains.

- Herbs and Spices: The Mediterranean region is known for its abundant use of herbs and spices, which add complexity and depth to dishes. Herbs like oregano, basil, rosemary, and thyme, along with spices like cinnamon, turmeric, and cumin, can transform simple ingredients into flavorful and aromatic meals. These natural flavor enhancers can be used generously to season proteins, vegetables, soups, and stews without adding extra calories or carbohydrates.

- Variety of Fresh Produce: The Diabetic Mediterranean Diet encourages a wide variety of fruits and vegetables, which provide an array of flavors and textures. By incorporating seasonal produce, individuals can enjoy the natural sweetness of ripe fruits and the savory flavors of vegetables. Roasting, grilling, or sautéing vegetables can bring out their natural flavors and caramelization, making them delicious and satisfying additions to meals.

- Lean Proteins: The diet includes lean sources of protein, such as skinless poultry, fish, and plant-based proteins like tofu and legumes. These

proteins can be prepared using various cooking techniques, such as grilling, baking, or stir-frying, to enhance their taste and texture. Marinating proteins with herbs, spices, and citrus juices can infuse them with additional flavor.

- Whole Grains and High-Fiber Carbohydrates: The Diabetic Mediterranean Diet incorporates whole grains like brown rice, quinoa, and whole wheat bread, which provide a nutty flavor and chewy texture to meals. High-fiber carbohydrates, such as legumes and fibrous vegetables, add bulk and satiety while contributing to stable blood sugar levels. These ingredients can be combined with herbs, spices, and healthy fats to create flavorful and satisfying dishes.

- Culinary Techniques: The Mediterranean diet offers a variety of culinary techniques that enhance flavors without relying on added sugars or excessive salt. Techniques like grilling, roasting, sautéing, and braising can bring out the natural flavors of ingredients, creating depth and complexity in dishes. These techniques can be combined with the use of herbs, spices, and healthy fats to create flavorful and well-balanced meals.

By combining the flavorsome elements of the Mediterranean diet with the specific considerations for managing diabetes, the Diabetic Mediterranean Diet offers a delicious and satisfying approach to eating. It demonstrates that a diabetic diet doesn't have to be bland or restrictive. Instead, it encourages the use of whole, unprocessed foods, healthy fats, and a variety of herbs and spices to create flavorful meals that support blood sugar control and overall well-being.

It's important to note that individual tastes and preferences may vary, and it's always advisable to consult with a registered dietitian or healthcare professional to tailor the diet to personal needs and ensure it aligns with specific diabetes management goals.

30-Day Meal Plan

Day 1

- **Breakfast:** Mediterranean Omelet
- **Lunch:** Provencal Lemon and Olive Chicken
- **Dinner:** Mashed Potatoes and Cauliflower with Sour Cream
- **Snack:** Yogurt & Honey Fruit Cups

Day 2

- **Breakfast:** Pulled Chicken Sandwiches
- **Lunch:** Spicy Beef & Pepper Stir-Fry
- **Dinner:** Mediterranean Pork & Orzo
- **Snack:** Fresh Is Best Hummus

Day 3

- **Breakfast:** Mediterranean Broccoli & Cheese Omelet
- **Lunch:** Skillet Pork Chops with Apples & Onion
- **Dinner:** Cod and Asparagus Bake
- **Snack:** Nutty White Bean Hummus

Day 4

- **Breakfast:** Mediterranean Tomato Bites
- **Lunch:** Ginger Steak Fried Rice
- **Dinner:** Mediterranean Chicken Pasta
- **Snack:** Greek Isle Mushroom Stuffers

Day 5

- **Breakfast:** Veggie Omelet with Goat Cheese
- **Lunch:** Grilled Beef Chimichangas
- **Dinner:** Green Bean and Red Pepper SautÉ
- **Snack:** Mediterranean Roasted Pepper Dip

Day 6

- **Breakfast:** Mediterranean Veggie Brunch Puff
- **Lunch:** In-A-Pinch Chicken & Spinach

- **Dinner:** Mediterranean Chicken
- **Snack:** Lemon Garlic Hummus

Day 7

- **Breakfast:** Mediterranean Veggie Brunch Puff
- **Lunch:** Peppered Tuna Kababs
- **Dinner:** Feta Shrimp Skillet
- **Snack:** Homemade Hummus

Day 8

- **Breakfast:** Feta Asparagus Frittata
- **Lunch:** Makeover Turkey Burgers with Peach Mayo
- **Dinner:** Creamy Pesto Spaghetti Squash
- **Snack:** Greek Salad Cracker Snack

Day 9

- **Breakfast:** Date & Pine Nut Overnight Oatmeal
- **Lunch:** Chicken, Mushroom, and Asiago Cheese Pizza
- **Dinner:** Lemony Roasted Shrimp and Asparagus
- **Snack:** 7-Layer Mediterranean Dip

Day 10

- **Breakfast:** Pineapple Green Smoothie
- **Lunch:** Mediterranean Baked Tuna
- **Dinner:** Dill Pickle Chicken
- **Snack:** Yogurt & Honey Fruit Cups

Day 11

- **Breakfast:** Creamy Blueberry-Pecan Overnight Oatmeal
- **Lunch:** Saucy Mediterranean Chicken with Rice
- **Dinner:** Greek Lamb Burgers
- **Snack:** Lemon Garlic Hummus

Day 12

- **Breakfast:** Everything Bagel Avocado Toast
- **Lunch:** Mediterranean Chicken Orzo Soup
- **Dinner:** Mediterranean Grilled Lamb Chops

- **Snack:** Fresh Is Best Hummus

Day 13

- **Breakfast:** Mediterranean Veggie Brunch Puff
- **Lunch:** Mediterranean Chickpeas
- **Dinner:** Pizzaiola Chops
- **Snack:** Homemade Hummus

Day 14

- **Breakfast:** Feta Asparagus Frittata
- **Lunch:** Veggie Couscous
- **Dinner:** Chili-Rubbed Steak with Black Bean Salad
- **Snack:** Nutty White Bean Hummus

Day 15

- **Breakfast:** Date & Pine Nut Overnight Oatmeal
- **Lunch:** Greek Roast Potatoes with Lemon and Garlic
- **Dinner:** Garlicky Mustard Lamb Chops
- **Snack:** Greek Salad Cracker Snack

Day 16

- **Breakfast:** Pineapple Green Smoothie
- **Lunch:** Sun-Dried Tomato Mediterranean Chicken
- **Dinner:** Foil-Packet Lamb Chops
- **Snack:** Greek Isle Mushroom Stuffers

Day 17

- **Breakfast:** Creamy Blueberry-Pecan Overnight Oatmeal
- **Lunch:** Riviera Chicken
- **Dinner:** Mediterranean Lamb Meatballs
- **Snack:** 7-Layer Mediterranean Dip

Day 18

- **Breakfast:** Everything Bagel Avocado Toast
- **Lunch:** Greek Chicken
- **Dinner:** Greek Festival Fish
- **Snack:** Mediterranean Roasted Pepper Dip

Day 19

- **Breakfast:** Muesli with Raspberries
- **Lunch:** Mediterranean Best Cooked Chicken
- **Dinner:** Tropical Chicken Cauliflower Rice Bowls
- **Snack:** Yogurt & Honey Fruit Cups

Day 20

- **Breakfast:** Mediterranean Omelet
- **Lunch:** Skillet Greek Chicken
- **Dinner:** Slow-Cooker Pork Chops
- **Snack:** Homemade Hummus

Day 21

- **Breakfast:** Pulled Chicken Sandwiches
- **Lunch:** Mediterranean Best Cooked Chicken
- **Dinner:** Sweet & Tangy Salmon with Green Beans
- **Snack:** Greek Isle Mushroom Stuffers

Day 22

- **Breakfast:** Mediterranean Broccoli & Cheese Omelet
- **Lunch:** Mediterranean Veggie Blend
- **Dinner:** Parmesan Chicken with Artichoke Hearts
- **Snack:** Lemon Garlic Hummus

Day 23

- **Breakfast:** Mediterranean Tomato Bites
- **Lunch:** Lemon Basil Couscous
- **Dinner:** Greek-Style Chicken Pittas
- **Snack:** Chopped Grilled Vegetable Bowl with Farro

Day 24

- **Breakfast:** Veggie Omelet with Goat Cheese
- **Lunch:** Greek Spinach Pie
- **Dinner:** Chickpea Pasta with Lemony-Parsley Pesto
- **Snack:** Nutty White Bean Hummus

Day 25

- **Breakfast:** Mediterranean Veggie Brunch Puff
- **Lunch:** Falafel Patties
- **Dinner:** Caprese Stuffed Portobello Mushrooms
- **Snack:** 7-Layer Mediterranean Dip

Day 26

- **Breakfast:** Muesli with Raspberries
- **Lunch:** Bourtheto Fish Stew
- **Dinner:** Herby Cod with Roasted Tomatoes
- **Snack:** Roasted Summer Vegetables

Day 27

- **Breakfast:** Everything Bagel Avocado Toast
- **Lunch:** Greek Style Zucchini Blossoms Stuffed with Bulgur
- **Dinner:** Slow-Cooker Pasta E Fagioli Soup Freezer Pack
- **Snack:** Lemon Garlic Hummus

Day 28

- **Breakfast:** Creamy Blueberry-Pecan Overnight Oatmeal
- **Lunch:** Dijon Salmon with Green Bean Pilaf
- **Dinner:** One-Pot Spinach, Chicken Sausage & Feta Pasta
- **Snack:** Greek Salad Cracker Snack

Day 29

- **Breakfast:** Date & Pine Nut Overnight Oatmeal
- **Lunch:** Instant Pot White Chicken Chili Freezer Pack
- **Dinner:** Chickpea & Quinoa Bowl with Roasted Red Pepper Sauce
- **Snack:** Nutty White Bean Hummus

Day 30

- **Breakfast:** Veggie Omelet with Goat Cheese
- **Lunch:** Stuffed Sweet Potato with Hummus Dressing
- **Dinner:** Lemon Dijon Lamb Chops
- **Snack:** 7-Layer Mediterranean Dip

Chapter 1: Breakfast

Mediterranean Omelet

Prep Time: 5 Mins   Cook Time: 10 Mins   Serves: 2

Ingredients:

- 8 large eggs
- 1/2 teaspoon salt
- 1/4 teaspoon pepper
- 1 cup salsa, divided
- 1/2 cup shredded cheddar cheese
- 4 whole wheat English muffins, split and toasted
- 1/4 cup reduced-fat spreadable cream cheese
- 1 medium ripe avocado, peeled and cubed
- 1/2 small lime
- Reduced-fat sour cream, optional

Directions:

1. In a large bowl, whisk eggs, salt and pepper. Place a large skillet coated with cooking spray over medium-high heat. Pour in egg mixture; cook and stir until eggs are thickened and no liquid egg remains. Add 1/2 cup salsa and cheese; stir gently until cheese is melted.

2. Spread cut sides of English muffins with cream cheese and remaining salsa. Top with scrambled eggs and avocado. Squeeze lime juice over tops. If desired, serve with sour cream.

Nutritional Value (Amount per Serving):

Calories: 845; Fat: 40.84; Carb: 95.48; Protein: 33.2

Pulled Chicken Sandwiches

Prep Time: 20 Mins   Cook Time: 4 Mins   Serves: 6

Ingredients:

- 1 medium onion, finely chopped
- 1 can (6 ounces) tomato paste
- 1/4 cup reduced-sodium chicken broth
- 2 tablespoons brown sugar
- 1 tablespoon cider vinegar
- 1 tablespoon yellow mustard
- 1 tablespoon Worcestershire sauce
- 2 garlic cloves, minced
- 2 teaspoons chili powder
- 3/4 teaspoon salt
- 1/8 teaspoon cayenne pepper
- 1-1/2 pounds boneless skinless chicken breasts
- 6 whole wheat hamburger buns, split

Directions:

1. In a small bowl, mix the first 11 ingredients. Place chicken in a 3-qt. slow cooker. Pour sauce over top.

2. Cook, covered, on low until chicken is tender, 4-5 hours. Remove chicken; cool slightly. Shred meat with 2 forks. Return to slow cooker; heat through. Serve on buns.

Nutritional Value (Amount per Serving):

Calories: 500; Fat: 17.93; Carb: 45.14; Protein: 38.63

Mediterranean Broccoli & Cheese Omelet

Prep Time: 10 Mins   Cook Time: 20 Mins   Serves: 4

Ingredients:

- 2-1/2 cups fresh broccoli florets
- 6 large egg, room temperature
- 1/4 cup 2% milk
- 1/2 teaspoon salt
- 1/4 teaspoon pepper
- 1/3 cup grated Romano cheese
- 1/3 cup sliced pitted Greek olives
- 1 tablespoon olive oil
- Shaved Romano cheese and minced fresh parsley

Directions:

1. Preheat broiler. In a large saucepan, place steamer basket over 1 in. of water. Place broccoli in basket. Bring water to a boil. Reduce heat to a simmer; steam, covered, until crisp-tender, 4-6 minutes.

2. In a large bowl, whisk eggs, milk, salt and pepper. Stir in cooked broccoli, grated cheese and olives. In a large cast-iron or other ovenproof skillet, heat oil over medium heat; pour in egg mixture. Cook, uncovered, until eggs are nearly set, 4-6 minutes.

3. Broil 3-4 in. from heat until eggs are completely set, 2-4 minutes. Let stand 5 minutes. Cut into wedges. Sprinkle with shaved cheese and parsley.

Nutritional Value (Amount per Serving):

Calories: 152; Fat: 12.87; Carb: 3.22; Protein: 6.17

Mediterranean Tomato Bites

Prep Time: 10 Mins   Cook Time: 15 Mins   Serves: 32

Ingredients:

- 1 package (17.3 ounces) frozen puff pastry, thawed
- 1-1/2 cups shredded Gouda cheese
- 6 plum tomatoes, thinly sliced
- 1/4 cup pitted ripe olives, coarsely chopped
- 1 cup crumbled feta cheese
- Minced fresh basil
- Minced fresh oregano

Directions:

1. Preheat oven to 400°F. Unfold puff pastry. Cut each sheet into 16 squares; place on parchment-lined baking sheets.

2. Sprinkle with Gouda cheese; top with tomatoes, olives and feta cheese. Bake until golden brown, 14-18 minutes. Sprinkle with herbs.

Nutritional Value (Amount per Serving):

Calories: 71; Fat: 5.78; Carb: 1.06; Protein: 3.7

Veggie Omelet with Goat Cheese

Prep Time: 10 Mins   Cook Time: 20 Mins   Serves: 2

Ingredients:

- 4 large eggs
- 1/4 cup whole milk
- 1/4 teaspoon salt
- 1/8 teaspoon pepper
- 4 teaspoons olive oil, divided
- 1 cup thinly sliced zucchini
- 4 small fresh mushrooms, chopped
- 1/4 cup finely chopped green pepper
- 1 cup fresh baby spinach
- 2 green onions, thinly sliced
- 2 garlic cloves, thinly sliced
- 1/4 cup crumbled goat cheese
- Additional thinly sliced green onions

Directions:

1. In a small bowl, whisk eggs, milk, salt and pepper. In a large nonstick skillet, heat 2 teaspoons oil over medium-high heat. Add zucchini, mushrooms and green pepper; cook and stir 3-5 minutes or until tender.

2. Add spinach, green onions and garlic; cook and stir 1-2 minutes longer or until spinach is wilted and garlic is tender. Transfer vegetable mixture to a small bowl. In same pan, heat remaining oil. Pour in egg mixture. Mixture should set immediately at edge.

3. As eggs set, push cooked portions toward the center, letting uncooked eggs flow underneath. When eggs are thickened and no liquid egg remains, spoon vegetable mixture on one side; sprinkle with cheese. Fold omelet

in half; cut in half and slide onto plates. Sprinkle with additional green onions.

Nutritional Value (Amount per Serving):

Calories: 460; Fat: 35.98; Carb: 16.94; Protein: 19.27

Mediterranean Veggie Brunch Puff

Prep Time: 25 Mins   Cook Time: 25 Mins   Serves: 8

Ingredients:

- 6 large eggs
- 2 large egg whites
- 1 cup 2% milk
- 1 garlic clove, minced
- 1/2 teaspoon salt
- 1/4 teaspoon pepper
- 5 cups cubed croissants (about 6 ounces)
- 3/4 cup chopped roasted sweet
- red peppers, divided
- 1/2 cup finely chopped sweet onion
- 1 package (10 ounces) frozen chopped spinach, thawed and squeezed dry
- 1 cup shredded cheddar cheese
- 1/2 cup crumbled feta cheese
- 3 tablespoons Greek vinaigrette

Directions:

1. In a large bowl, whisk the first 6 ingredients until blended. Place croissant pieces in a single layer in a greased 11x7-in. baking dish; top with 1/2 cup red pepper, onion and spinach. Pour egg mixture over top. Sprinkle with cheeses. Refrigerate, covered, overnight.

2. Finely chop remaining red pepper; place in a jar with a tight-fitting lid. Add vinaigrette and shake to combine. Refrigerate until serving.

3. Preheat oven to 350°F. Remove casserole from refrigerator while oven heats. Bake, uncovered, 25-30 minutes or until a knife inserted in the center comes out clean. Let stand 5-10 minutes before cutting. Serve with vinaigrette mixture.

Nutritional Value (Amount per Serving):

Calories: 257; Fat: 12.6; Carb: 20.54; Protein: 16.01

Feta Asparagus Frittata

Prep Time: 10 Mins   Cook Time: 30 Mins   Serves: 2

Ingredients:

- 12 fresh asparagus spears, trimmed
- 6 large eggs
- 2 tablespoons heavy whipping cream
- Dash salt
- Dash pepper
- 1 tablespoon olive oil
- 2 green onions, chopped
- 1 garlic clove, minced
- 1/2 cup crumbled feta cheese

Directions:

1. Preheat oven to 350°F. In a large skillet, place asparagus in 1/2 in. water; bring to a boil. Cook, covered, until asparagus is crisp-tender, 3-5 minutes; drain. Cool slightly.

2. In a bowl, whisk together eggs, cream, salt and pepper. Chop 2 asparagus spears. In an 8-in. cast-iron or other ovenproof skillet, heat oil over medium heat until hot. Saute green onions, garlic and chopped asparagus for 1 minute. Stir in egg mixture; cook, covered, over medium heat until eggs are nearly set, 3-5 minutes. Top with whole asparagus spears and cheese.

3. Bake until eggs are completely set, 7-9 minutes.

Nutritional Value (Amount per Serving):

Calories: 409; Fat: 34.23; Carb: 11.3; Protein: 15.42

Date & Pine Nut Overnight Oatmeal

Prep Time: 10 Mins   Cook Time: 7 Hrs 5 Mins   Serves: 1

Ingredients:

- ½ cup old-fashioned rolled oats
- ½ cup water
- Pinch of salt
- 2 tablespoons chopped dates
- 1 tablespoon toasted pine nuts
- 1 teaspoon honey
- ¼ teaspoon ground cinnamon

Directions:

1. Combine oats, water and salt in a jar or bowl and stir. Cover and refrigerate overnight.

2. In the morning, heat the oats, if desired, or eat cold. Top with dates, pine nuts, honey and cinnamon.

Nutritional Value (Amount per Serving):

Calories: 180; Fat: 3.5; Carb: 48.22; Protein: 8.56

Pineapple Green Smoothie

Prep Time: 5 Mins   Cook Time: 5 Mins   Serves: 1

Ingredients:

- ½ cup unsweetened almond milk
- ⅓ cup nonfat plain Greek yogurt
- 1 cup baby spinach
- 1 cup frozen banana slices (about 1 medium banana)
- ½ cup frozen pineapple chunks
- 1 tablespoon chia seeds
- 1-2 teaspoons pure maple syrup or honey (optional)

Directions:

1. Add almond milk and yogurt to a blender, then add spinach, banana, pineapple, chia seeds and sweetener (if using); blend until smooth.

Nutritional Value (Amount per Serving):

Calories: 614; Fat: 11.03; Carb: 126.19; Protein: 13.87

Creamy Blueberry-Pecan Overnight Oatmeal

Prep Time: 10 Mins   Cook Time: 8 Hrs   Serves: 1

Ingredients:

- ½ cup old-fashioned rolled oats
- ½ cup water
- Pinch of salt
- ½ cup blueberries, fresh or frozen, thawed
- 2 tablespoons nonfat plain Greek yogurt
- 1 tablespoon toasted chopped pecans
- 2 teaspoons pure maple syrup

Directions:

1. Combine oats, water and salt in a jar or bowl. Cover and refrigerate overnight. In the morning, heat if desired, and top with blueberries, yogurt, pecans and syrup.

Nutritional Value (Amount per Serving):

Calories: 512; Fat: 10.25; Carb: 81.28; Protein: 44.25

Everything Bagel Avocado Toast

Prep Time: 5 Mins   Cook Time: 5 Mins   Serves: 1

Ingredients:

- ¼ medium avocado, mashed
- 1 slice whole-grain bread, toasted
- 2 teaspoons everything bagel seasoning
- Pinch of flaky sea salt (such as Maldon)

Directions:

1.Spread avocado on toast. Top with seasoning and salt.

Nutritional Value (Amount per Serving):

Calories: 683; Fat: 12.11; Carb: 118.77; Protein: 26.51

Muesli with Raspberries

Prep Time: 5 Mins   Cook Time: 5 Mins   Serves: 1 3/4

Ingredients:

- ⅓ cup muesli
- 1 cup raspberries
- ¾ cup low-fat milk

Directions:

1.Top muesli with raspberries and serve with milk.

Nutritional Value (Amount per Serving):

Calories: 543; Fat: 21.69; Carb: 60.49; Protein: 30.04

Chapter 2: Lunch

Provencal Lemon and Olive Chicken

Prep Time: 15 Mins   Cook Time: 3 1/2 Hrs   Serves: 10

Ingredients:

- 2 cups chopped onion
- 2 pounds skinless chicken thighs
- 1 medium lemon, thinly sliced and seeded
- 1/2 cup pitted green olives
- 1 tablespoon white vinegar or olive brine
- 2 teaspoons herbes de Provence
- 1 bay leaf
- 1/2 teaspoon salt
- 1/8 teaspoon black pepper
- 1 cup fat-free reduced-sodium chicken broth
- 1/2 cup minced fresh parsley

Directions:

1. Place onions in slow cooker. Arrange chicken thighs and lemon slices over onion. Add olives, vinegar, herbes de Provence, bay leaf, salt, and pepper. Pour in broth.

2. Cover; cook on LOW 5 to 6 hours or on HIGH 3 to 3 1/2 hours or until chicken is tender. Remove and discard bay leaf. Stir in parsley before serving.

Nutritional Value (Amount per Serving):

Calories: 225; Fat: 10.84; Carb: 10.2; Protein: 21.19

Spicy Beef & Pepper Stir-Fry

Prep Time: 20 Mins   Cook Time: 10 Mins   Serves: 4

Ingredients:

- 1 pound beef top sirloin steak, cut into thin strips
- 1 tablespoon minced fresh gingerroot
- 3 garlic cloves, minced, divided
- 1/4 teaspoon pepper
- 3/4 teaspoon salt, divided
- 1 cup light coconut milk
- 2 tablespoons sugar
- 1 tablespoon Sriracha chili sauce
- 1/2 teaspoon grated lime zest
- 2 tablespoons lime juice
- 2 tablespoons canola oil, divided
- 1 large sweet red pepper, cut into thin strips
- 1/2 medium red onion, thinly sliced
- 1 jalapeno pepper, seeded and thinly sliced
- 4 cups fresh baby spinach
- 2 green onions, thinly sliced
- 2 tablespoons chopped fresh cilantro

Directions:

1. In a large bowl, toss beef with ginger, 2 garlic cloves, pepper and 1/2 teaspoon salt; let stand 15 minutes. Meanwhile, in a small bowl, whisk coconut milk, sugar, chili sauce, lime zest, lime juice and remaining 1/4 tsp. salt until blended.

2. In a large skillet, heat 1 tablespoon oil over medium-high heat. Add beef; stir-fry until no longer pink, 2-3 minutes. Remove from pan.

3. Stir-fry red pepper, red onion, jalapeno and remaining clove of garlic in remaining 1 Tbsp. oil just until vegetables are crisp-tender, 2-3 minutes. Stir in coconut milk mixture; heat through. Add spinach and beef; cook until spinach is wilted and beef is heated through, stirring occasionally. Sprinkle with green onions and cilantro.

Nutritional Value (Amount per Serving):

Calories: 507; Fat: 37.36; Carb: 15.8; Protein: 28.83

Skillet Pork Chops with Apples & Onion

Prep Time: 10 Mins   Cook Time: 10 Mins   Serves: 4

Ingredients:

- 4 boneless pork loin chops (6 ounces each)
- 3 medium apples, cut into wedges
- 1 large onion, cut into thin wedges
- 1/4 cup water
- 1/3 cup balsamic vinaigrette
- 1/2 teaspoon salt
- 1/4 teaspoon pepper

Directions:

1. Place a large nonstick skillet over medium heat; brown pork chops on both sides, about 4 minutes. Remove from pan.

2. In same skillet, combine apples, onion and water. Place pork chops over apple mixture; drizzle chops with vinaigrette. Sprinkle with salt and pepper. Reduce heat; simmer, covered, until a thermometer inserted in chops reads 145°, 3-5 minutes.

Nutritional Value (Amount per Serving):

Calories: 324; Fat: 6.62; Carb: 23; Protein: 42.38

Ginger Steak Fried Rice

Prep Time: 10 Mins   Cook Time: 20 Mins   Serves: 4

Ingredients:

- 2 large eggs, lightly beaten
- 2 teaspoons olive oil
- 1 beef top sirloin steak (3/4 pound), cut into thin strips
- 4 tablespoons reduced-sodium soy sauce, divided
- 1 package (12 ounces) broccoli
- coleslaw mix
- 1 cup frozen peas
- 2 tablespoons grated fresh gingerroot
- 3 garlic cloves, minced
- 2 cups cooked brown rice
- 4 green onions, sliced

Directions:

1. In a large skillet coated with cooking spray, cook and stir eggs over medium heat until no liquid egg remains, break up eggs into small pieces. Remove from pan; wipe skillet clean if necessary.

2. In same pan, heat oil over medium-high heat. Add beef; stir-fry.

3. 1-2 minutes or until no longer pink. Stir in 1 tablespoon soy sauce; remove from pan.

4. Add coleslaw mix, peas, ginger and garlic to the pan; cook and stir until coleslaw mix is crisp-tender. Add rice and remaining soy sauce, tossing to combine rice with vegetable mixture; heat through. Stir in cooked eggs, beef and green onions; heat through.

Nutritional Value (Amount per Serving):

Calories: 404; Fat: 22.4; Carb: 12.81; Protein: 36.58

Grilled Beef Chimichangas

Prep Time: 25 Mins   Cook Time: 10 Mins   Serves: 6

Ingredients:

- 1 pound lean ground beef (90% lean)
- 1 small onion, chopped
- 2 garlic cloves, minced
- 1 can (4 ounces) chopped green chilies
- 1/4 cup salsa
- 1/4 teaspoon ground cumin
- 6 whole wheat tortillas (8 inches)
- 3/4 cup shredded Monterey Jack cheese
- Reduced-fat sour cream and guacamole, optional

Directions:

1. In a large skillet, cook beef, onion and garlic over medium heat 6-8 minutes or until beef is no longer pink and onion is tender, breaking up beef into crumbles; drain. Stir in chilies, salsa and cumin.

2. Spoon 1/2 cup beef mixture across center of each tortilla; top with 2 tablespoons cheese. Fold bottom and sides of tortilla over filling and roll up.

3. Place chimichangas on grill rack, seam side down. Grill, covered, over medium-low heat 10-12 minutes or until crisp and browned, turning once. If desired, serve with sour cream and guacamole.

Nutritional Value (Amount per Serving):

Calories: 393; Fat: 17.51; Carb: 28.16; Protein: 29.89

In-A-Pinch Chicken & Spinach

Prep Time: 10 Mins   Cook Time: 15 Mins   Serves: 4

Ingredients:

- 4 boneless skinless chicken breast halves (6 ounces each)
- 2 tablespoons olive oil
- 1 tablespoon butter
- 1 package (6 ounces) fresh baby spinach
- 1 cup salsa

Directions:

1. Pound chicken with a meat mallet to 1/2-in. thickness. In a large skillet, heat oil and butter over medium heat. Cook chicken until no longer pink, 5-6 minutes on each side. Remove and keep warm.

2. Add spinach and salsa to pan; cook and stir until spinach is just wilted, 3-4 minutes. Serve with chicken.

Nutritional Value (Amount per Serving):

Calories: 404; Fat: 16.2; Carb: 6.95; Protein: 56.16

Peppered Tuna Kababs

Prep Time: 10 Mins   Cook Time: 20 Mins   Serves: 4

Ingredients:

- 1/2 cup frozen corn, thawed
- 4 green onions, chopped
- 1 jalapeno pepper, seeded and chopped
- 2 tablespoons coarsely chopped fresh parsley
- 2 tablespoons lime juice
- 1 pound tuna steaks, cut into
- 1-inch cubes
- 1 teaspoon coarsely ground pepper
- 2 large sweet red peppers, cut into 2x1-inch pieces
- 1 medium mango, peeled and cut into 1-inch cubes

Directions:

1. For salsa, in a small bowl, combine the first five ingredients; set aside.

2. Rub tuna with pepper. On four metal or soaked wooden skewers, alternately thread red peppers, tuna and mango.

3. Place skewers on greased grill rack. Cook, covered, over medium heat, turning occasionally, until tuna is slightly pink in center (medium-rare) and peppers are tender, 10-12 minutes. Serve with salsa.

Nutritional Value (Amount per Serving):

Calories: 327; Fat: 8.69; Carb: 54.72; Protein: 9.36

Makeover Turkey Burgers with Peach Mayo

Prep Time: 10 Mins   Cook Time: 15 Mins   Serves: 6

Ingredients:

- 1-1/2 teaspoons canola oil
- 2 small peaches, peeled and chopped
- 1/2 teaspoon minced fresh gingerroot
- 4 teaspoons reduced-sodium teriyaki sauce, divided
- 1/4 cup chopped red onion
- 1/2 teaspoon pepper
- 1/4 teaspoon salt
- 1-1/2 pounds lean ground turkey
- 1/3 cup fat-free mayonnaise
- 6 multigrain hamburger buns, split and toasted
- Optional toppings: lettuce leaves and slices of peaches, red onion and tomatoes

Directions:

1. In a skillet, heat oil over medium-high heat. Add peaches and ginger; cook and stir until peaches are tender. Stir in 1 teaspoon teriyaki sauce; cook 1 minute longer. Transfer to a small bowl; cool slightly.

2. In a large bowl, combine onion, pepper, salt and remaining teriyaki sauce.

Add turkey; mix lightly but thoroughly. Shape into six 1/2-in.-thick patties.

3. Moisten a paper towel with cooking oil; using long-handled tongs, rub on grill rack to coat lightly. Grill burgers, covered, over medium heat or broil 4 in. from heat 5-6 minutes on each side, or until a thermometer reads 165°.

4. Stir mayonnaise into peach mixture. Serve burgers on buns with peach mayo and toppings as desired.

Nutritional Value (Amount per Serving):

Calories: 313; Fat: 8.17; Carb: 38.78; Protein: 22.09

Chicken, Mushroom, and Asiago Cheese Pizza

Prep Time: 10 Mins   Cook Time: 20 Mins   Serves: 6

Ingredients:

- 2 tablespoons light balsamic vinaigrette
- 1 medium onion, thinly sliced
- 1 package (8 ounces) sliced mushrooms
- 1 (10 1/2-ounce) stone-baked or whole wheat pizza crust
- 1 cup (about 8 ounces) shredded cooked skinless chicken breast
- 3/4 cup shredded Asiago cheese

Directions:

1. Heat oven to 400°F. Heat dressing in large skillet on medium-high heat. Add onion and cook 5 minutes; stirring occasionally. Add mushrooms and cook an additional 5 minutes; stirring occasionally.

2. Spread onion mixture evenly over pizza crust. Top with chicken and cheese.

3. Bake 15 to 20 minutes or until crust is crisp.

Nutritional Value (Amount per Serving):

Calories: 136; Fat: 4.71; Carb: 9.63; Protein: 14.11

Mediterranean Baked Tuna

Prep Time: 10 Mins   Cook Time: 12 Mins   Serves: 4

Ingredients:

- 2 tablespoons olive oil, divided
- 4 (4-ounce) tuna steaks (1/2-inch-thick)
- 2 teaspoons balsamic vinegar
- 2 teaspoons dried rosemary
- 1/4 teaspoon crushed red pepper

- 1/4 teaspoon salt
- 2 plum tomatoes, chopped

Directions:

1. Preheat the oven to 350 degrees.

2. Sprinkle 1 tablespoon oil over the bottom of a 9- x 13-inch baking dish. Place the tuna in the baking dish and sprinkle with the remaining 1 tablespoon oil and the balsamic vinegar. Sprinkle the rosemary, red pepper, and salt evenly over the tuna.

3. Top the tuna with the tomatoes and bake for 12 to 15 minutes, or until the tuna is cooked to desired doneness.

Nutritional Value (Amount per Serving):

Calories: 577; Fat: 39.52; Carb: 5.88; Protein: 46.96

Saucy Mediterranean Chicken with Rice

Prep Time: 10 Mins   Cook Time: 20 Mins   Serves: 4

Ingredients:

- 3/4 cup water
- 3 tablespoons tomato paste
- 2 tablespoons lemon juice
- 3/4 teaspoon salt
- 1 teaspoon chili powder
- 1/2 teaspoon garlic powder
- 1/2 teaspoon ground ginger
- 1/4 teaspoon ground fennel seed
- 1/4 teaspoon ground turmeric
- 1 teaspoon ground coriander, optional
- 3 tablespoons olive oil
- 1 medium onion, chopped
- 1 pound boneless skinless chicken breasts, cut into 1-inch cubes
- 3 cups hot cooked rice
- Minced fresh parsley, optional

Directions:

1. In a small bowl, mix the water, tomato paste, lemon juice, salt, chili powder, garlic powder, ginger, fennel, turmeric and, if desired, coriander until smooth.

2. In a large skillet, heat oil over medium-high heat. Add onions; cook and stir until tender. Stir in chicken; brown 3-4 minutes. Pour water mixture into pan.

3. Bring to a boil. Reduce heat; simmer, uncovered, until chicken is no longer pink, 8-10 minutes. Serve with rice. If desired, top with parsley.

Nutritional Value (Amount per Serving):

Calories: 538; Fat: 31.9; Carb: 51.28; Protein: 38.84

Mediterranean Chicken Orzo Soup

Prep Time: 20 Mins   Cook Time: 25 Mins   Serves: 6

Ingredients:

- 2 tablespoons olive oil, divided
- 3/4 pound boneless skinless chicken breasts, cubed
- 2 celery ribs, chopped
- 2 medium carrots, chopped
- 1 small onion, chopped
- 1/2 teaspoon salt
- 1/2 teaspoon dried oregano
- 1/4 teaspoon pepper
- 1/4 cup white wine or additional reduced-sodium chicken broth
- 1 carton (32 ounces) reduced-sodium chicken broth
- 1 teaspoon minced fresh rosemary
- 1 bay leaf
- 1 cup uncooked whole wheat orzo pasta
- 1 teaspoon grated lemon zest
- 1 tablespoon lemon juice
- Minced fresh parsley, optional

Directions:

1. In a large saucepan, heat 1 tablespoon oil over medium-high heat. Add chicken; cook and stir 6-8 minutes or until no longer pink. Remove from pan.

2. In same pan, heat remaining oil over medium-high heat. Add vegetables, salt, oregano and pepper; cook and stir 4-6 minutes or until vegetables are crisp-tender. Add wine, stirring to loosen browned bits from pan. Stir in broth, rosemary and bay leaf; bring to a boil.

3. Add orzo. Reduce heat; simmer, covered, 15-18 minutes or until orzo is tender, stirring occasionally. Return chicken to pan; heat through. Stir in lemon zest and juice; remove bay leaf. If desired, top each serving with parsley.

Nutritional Value (Amount per Serving):

Calories: 291; Fat: 15.38; Carb: 14.42; Protein: 25.1

Mediterranean Chickpeas

Prep Time: 10 Mins   Cook Time: 15 Mins   Serves: 4

Ingredients:

- 1 cup water
- 3/4 cup uncooked whole wheat couscous
- 1 tablespoon olive oil
- 1 medium onion, chopped
- 2 garlic cloves, minced

- 1 can (15 ounces) chickpeas or garbanzo beans, rinsed and drained
- 1 can (14-1/2 ounces) no-salt-added stewed tomatoes, cut up
- 1 can (14 ounces) water-packed artichoke hearts, rinsed, drained and chopped
- 1/2 cup pitted Greek olives, coarsely chopped
- 1 tablespoon lemon juice
- 1/2 teaspoon dried oregano
- Dash pepper
- Dash cayenne pepper

Directions:

1. In a small saucepan, bring water to a boil. Stir in couscous. Remove from heat; let stand, covered, 5-10 minutes or until water is absorbed. Fluff with a fork.

2. Meanwhile, in a large nonstick skillet, heat oil over medium-high heat. Add onion; cook and stir until tender. Add garlic; cook 1 minute longer. Sir in remaining ingredients; heat through, stirring occasionally. Serve with couscous.

Nutritional Value (Amount per Serving):

Calories: 204; Fat: 7.49; Carb: 30.09; Protein: 7.21

Veggie Couscous

Prep Time: 10 Mins   Cook Time: 20 Mins   Serves: 3

Ingredients:

- 2 tablespoons olive oil
- 1 small onion, finely chopped
- 1 carrot, diced
- 1 small zucchini, diced
- 2 garlic cloves, minced
- 1 3/4 cup chicken broth
- 1/4 cup water
- 1/2 teaspoon salt
- 1 (10-ounce) package couscous

Directions:

1. In a large saucepan, heat oil over medium-high heat. Add onion, carrot, zucchini, and garlic, and sauté 10 to 12 minutes, or until tender. Stir in broth, water, and salt; bring to a boil.

2. Stir in couscous; cover and remove from heat. Allow to sit, covered, for 5 minutes. Fluff with a fork then serve.

Nutritional Value (Amount per Serving):

Calories: 381; Fat: 18.87; Carb: 18.13; Protein: 32.91

Greek Roast Potatoes with Lemon and Garlic

Prep Time: 10 Mins   Cook Time: 20 Mins   Serves: 4

Ingredients:

- 2 pounds all-purpose potatoes, peeled and cut into wedges
- 2 tablespoons extra virgin olive oil
- 1/3 cup lemon juice, fresh or bottled
- 3 cloves garlic, sliced thin
- 1 teaspoon oregano, dried (or 2 teaspoons fresh)
- 1/2 teaspoon turmeric
- 1 1/2 cup low-sodium vegetable or chicken stock
- 1/2 teaspoon kosher salt
- 1/4 teaspoon black pepper, ground

Directions:

1. Peel and cut the potatoes, placing them in water while you do so. Preheat oven to 375 degrees F.

2. Combine the drained potatoes, olive oil, lemon juice, garlic, oregano, and turmeric in a large mixing bowl and marinate for 10 minutes.

3. Place potatoes in a large roasting pan with marinade, stock, salt, and pepper. Roast uncovered for approximately 55 minutes, turning occasionally, until potatoes are tender and lightly browned.

Nutritional Value (Amount per Serving):

Calories: 925; Fat: 7.12; Carb: 183.66; Protein: 28.36

Sun-Dried Tomato Mediterranean Chicken

Prep Time: 10 Mins   Cook Time: 20 Mins   Serves: 4

Ingredients:

- 4 (4-ounce) boneless, skinless chicken breast halves, rinsed and patted dry
- 1/3 cup thinly sliced sun-dried tomatoes in oil
- 1 tablespoon sun-dried tomato oil
- 1/3 cup chopped ripe olives
- 1/3 cup grated Parmesan cheese

Directions:

1. Preheat oven to 450 degrees F. Cut 4 (12-inch) squares of foil. Fold each square in half diagonally to crease, then open up foil and lay flat.

2. Rub chicken breast halves with oil from sun-dried tomatoes. Spoon 1

tablespoon tomatoes, 1 tablespoon olives, and 1 tablespoon cheese over each chicken breast half. Loosely fold foil over chicken and seal edges.

3. Bake 15 minutes, then check chicken for doneness. (Be careful when opening steaming packets.) If chicken is still pink, reseal and bake for about 5 additional minutes, or until chicken is no longer pink.

Nutritional Value (Amount per Serving):

Calories: 946; Fat: 33.62; Carb: 109.44; Protein: 49.61

Riviera Chicken

Prep Time: 10 Mins   Cook Time: 20 Mins   Serves: 4

Ingredients:

- 4 (4-ounce) boneless skinless chicken breast halves, rinsed and patted dry
- 1/8 teaspoon salt
- 1/8 teaspoon black pepper
- 1 can (14.5-ounce) diced tomatoes with basil, garlic, and oregano
- 1/2 cup drained, sliced black olives
- 1 tablespoon finely grated lemon peel
- ● 2 cloves garlic, chopped

Directions:

1. Coat a medium nonstick skillet with cooking spray. Heat to medium-high heat.

2. Sprinkle chicken with salt and pepper. Place in skillet, cover, and cook 5 to 7 minutes on each side, or until no longer pink. Remove chicken from skillet. Reduce heat to medium.

3. Add tomatoes, olives, lemon peel, and garlic to skillet. Cook about 4 minutes, or until hot, stirring occasionally. Return chicken to skillet and heat through.

Nutritional Value (Amount per Serving):

Calories: 333; Fat: 8.24; Carb: 7.6; Protein: 53.87

Greek Chicken

Prep Time: 10 Mins   Cook Time: 20 Mins   Serves: 6

Ingredients:

- 1 tablespoon vegetable oil
- 6 boneless, skinless chicken breast cutlets (4 ounces each)
- 1/2 teaspoon salt
- 1/4 teaspoon black pepper
- 1 (12-ounce) jar chicken gravy
- 1/4 cup dry white wine
- 1 1/2 teaspoon fresh lemon juice
- 1 1/2 teaspoon dried oregano
- 2 tablespoons sliced black olives (optional)
- 1/4 cup crumbled feta cheese (optional)

Directions:

1. In a large skillet, heat the oil over medium-high heat. Season the chicken with the salt and pepper, then brown for 3 to 4 minutes per side.

2. In a small bowl, combine the gravy, wine, lemon juice, and oregano; mix well. Pour over the chicken, and simmer for 4 to 5 minutes, or until no pink remains in the chicken. Top with olives and feta cheese, if desired, and serve.

Nutritional Value (Amount per Serving):

Calories: 952; Fat: 34.39; Carb: 108.1; Protein: 50.37

Mediterranean Best Cooked Chicken

Prep Time: 10 Mins   Cook Time: 35 Mins   Serves: 4

Ingredients:

- 2 tablespoons olive oil
- 1 pound boneless, skinless chicken breasts, cut into 1-inch chunks
- 1 teaspoon dried basil
- 1 garlic clove, minced
- 1/2 a small onion, diced
- 1/2 a small green bell pepper, diced
- 1/2 a small red bell pepper, diced
- 1/3 cup dry white wine
- 1 can (14.5 ounces) diced tomatoes
- 1/4 cup sliced pimiento-stuffed green olives
- 1/4 teaspoon black pepper

Directions:

1. In a large skillet, heat the oil over medium heat. Add the chicken and basil to the skillet and brown the chicken, stirring frequently.

2. Add the remaining ingredients and cook, uncovered, for 20 minutes, or until the vegetables are tender, no pink remains in the chicken, and the juices run clear.

Nutritional Value (Amount per Serving):

Calories: 324; Fat: 16.4; Carb: 30.12; Protein: 14.49

Skillet Greek Chicken

Prep Time: 10 Mins   Cook Time: 30 Mins   Serves: 5

Ingredients:

- 2 tablespoons olive oil
- 3 tablespoons lemon juice, divided
- 2 tablespoons chopped fresh parsley, divided
- 2 teaspoons dried oregano
- 1/4 teaspoon black pepper
- 1 (3-pound) chicken, cut into 8 pieces and skin removed
- 1/2 cup crumbled fat-free feta cheese

Directions:

1. In a medium bowl, combine the olive oil, 2 tablespoons lemon juice, 1 tablespoon parsley, the oregano, and pepper; mix well. Add the chicken and turn to coat evenly.

2. Heat a large skillet over high heat; brown the chicken for 5 to 6 minutes per side then reduce the heat to low, cover, and simmer for 10 minutes.

3. Add the remaining 1 tablespoon each of lemon juice and parsley, and the feta cheese; cover and simmer for 5 minutes, or until the cheese softens and the chicken is no longer pink.

Nutritional Value (Amount per Serving):

Calories: 294; Fat: 10.9; Carb: 3.3; Protein: 43.44

Mediterranean Veggie Blend

Prep Time: 10 Mins   Cook Time: 25 Mins   Serves: 2

Ingredients:

- 1 eggplant, peeled and cut into 1-inch cubes
- 2 cups zucchini slices
- 2 cups sliced small white mushrooms
- 1 (15-ounce) can diced tomatoes with basil, oregano, and garlic

Directions:

1. Coat a large nonstick skillet with cooking spray. Over medium heat, cook eggplant, zucchini, and mushrooms about 5 minutes.

2. Add tomatoes to skillet and bring to a boil. Reduce heat to low and simmer about 20 minutes, or until vegetables are tender, stirring occasionally.

Nutritional Value (Amount per Serving):

Calories: 127; Fat: 1.05; Carb: 28.12; Protein: 3.99

Lemon Basil Couscous

Prep Time: 10 Mins   Cook Time: 30 Mins   Serves: 4

Ingredients:

- 1 (10-ounce) package couscous
- 1 (15-ounce) can garbanzo beans (chick peas), drained and rinsed
- 1/4 cup chopped fresh basil
- 1/2 of a medium-sized red onion, chopped
- 1 medium-sized tomato, chopped
- 1/2 cup lemon juice
- 1 1/2 teaspoon salt
- 1/2 teaspoon black pepper

Directions:

1. Prepare couscous according to package directions. Place couscous in a large bowl to cool.

2. Add remaining ingredients; toss until well combined. Cover and chill for at least 1 hour before serving.

Nutritional Value (Amount per Serving):

Calories: 144; Fat: 0.92; Carb: 28.28; Protein: 7.18

Greek Spinach Pie

Prep Time: 10 Mins   Cook Time: 1 Hr 30 Mins   Serves: 6

Ingredients:

- 1 (10-ounce) container refrigerated pizza dough
- 1 small onion, chopped
- 1 clove garlic, minced
- 1/2 teaspoon dried basil
- 3/4 cup low-fat cottage cheese
- 3 ounces low-fat crumbled feta cheese
- 3/4 cup evaporated skim milk
- 8 egg whites
- 2 (10-ounce) packages frozen chopped spinach, thawed and squeezed dry

Directions:

1. Preheat the oven to 350 degrees F. Coat a 9-inch pie plate with nonstick cooking spray.

2. Unroll the pizza dough and form into a ball. On a lightly floured surface, slightly flatten the dough with your hands, then roll out the dough to form a 12-inch circle. Place in the pie plate to form a crust.

3. Lightly coat a medium skillet with nonstick cooking spray. Add the onion, garlic, and basil. Cook over medium heat for 3 to 4 minutes, or until the onion is tender, stirring constantly.

4. In a large bowl, beat together the cottage cheese and feta cheese until creamy and well mixed. Add the evaporated milk and egg whites and continue beating until well combined. Stir in the onion mixture and spinach.

5. Pour the mixture into the pie crust. Bake for 55 to 60 minutes, or until a knife inserted in the center comes out clean. Let stand for 15 minutes, then cut into wedges and serve.

Nutritional Value (Amount per Serving):

Calories: 215; Fat: 8.62; Carb: 16.55; Protein: 19.19

Falafel Patties

Prep Time: 10 Mins   Cook Time: 30 Mins   Serves: 8

Ingredients:

- 2 (15-ounce) cans chick peas, drained and rinsed
- 1/2 cup dry bread crumbs
- 1/2 cup fresh chopped parsley
- 1 small onion, minced
- 2 cloves garlic, minced
- 1 egg
- 1 teaspoon fresh lemon juice
- 2 tablespoons water
- 1 teaspoon ground cumin
- 1/8 teaspoon ground red pepper
- 1/4 teaspoon salt
- 1/4 teaspoon black pepper

Directions:

1. In a food processor fitted with its metal cutting blade, process all the ingredients until thoroughly combined. Cover and chill for 30 minutes.

2. Shape the mixture into 24 patties, about 2 inches wide and 1/2 inch thick.

3. Coat a large skillet with nonstick cooking spray. Heat the skillet over medium heat. Add the patties in batches and cook for 3 minutes per side, or until crispy and golden. Serve warm.

Nutritional Value (Amount per Serving):

Calories: 138; Fat: 3.24; Carb: 21.1; Protein: 6.82

Bourtheto Fish Stew

Prep Time: 5 Mins   Cook Time: 30 Mins   Serves: 2-4

Ingredients:

- 4 cod fillets
- 1 1/4 cups onion, sliced (or diced if you like)
- 1 cup water
- 1/4 cup olive oil
- 1/2 teaspoon paprika
- 1/8 teaspoon cayenne
- 1 teaspoon salt
- 1 teaspoon pepper

Directions:

1.In pan add: water, olive oil, onions, paprika, cayenne, salt and pepper.

2.Bring to boil, reduce heat and simmer for 10-15min, until onions soften.

3.Add cod and continue simmering for another 10-15min or until fish is done.

4.Place desired number of fish in each dish, top with onion mixture.

5.Serve!

Nutritional Value (Amount per Serving):

Calories: 292; Fat: 18.78; Carb: 6.15; Protein: 24.51

Greek Style Zucchini Blossoms Stuffed with Bulgur

Prep Time: 10 Mins   Cook Time: 20 Mins   Serves: 2-4

Ingredients:

- 1 cup olive oil
- 1 cup, chopped onion
- 1 cup, chopped chives
- 3 cloves, minced garlic
- 1 cup, grated zucchini
- 1 cup bulgur (cracked wheat)
- 2/3 cup (optional) raisins
- 1/2-1 teaspoon chili pepper
- 1 1/2 cups water
- 1/2 cup (optional) pine nuts
- 3 tablespoons, chopped fresh mint leaves
- 1/2-2/3 cup, chopped parsley or dill
- Pepper
- Salt
- 20 -25 zucchini blossoms
- 3 cups yogurt

Directions:

1.Preheat the oven to 375 degrees F.

2.In a deep skillet, heat half the oil over medium heat and sauté the onion, chives, and garlic until soft, about 5 minutes.

3. Add the zucchini, bulgur, raisins, chili pepper, and 1 cup water. Reduce the heat and simmer for 10 minutes. Add a little more water if all is absorbed.

4. Turn off the heat and add the pine nuts, mint, and dill to the stuffing. Season with salt, stir, and taste. Add more salt and pepper if needed.

5. Using a spoon, carefully stuff each blossom.

6. Fold the top over and place on their sides, very closely together, in an earthenware casserole.

7. Pour the remaining olive oil and 1/2 cup water.

8. Cover the dish and place in the oven.

9. Bake for about 1 hour, checking periodically to see if a little more water is needed, until most of the liquid has been absorbed.

10. Serve hot or cold, accompanied by yogurt.

Nutritional Value (Amount per Serving):

Calories: 682; Fat: 33.02; Carb: 80.45; Protein: 33.22

Dijon Salmon with Green Bean Pilaf

Prep Time: 30 Mins   Cook Time: 30 Mins   Serves: 4

Ingredients:

- 1 ¼ pounds wild salmon (see Tip), skinned and cut into 4 portions
- 3 tablespoons extra-virgin olive oil, divided
- 1 tablespoon minced garlic
- ¾ teaspoon salt
- 2 tablespoons mayonnaise
- 2 teaspoons whole-grain mustard
- ½ teaspoon ground pepper, divided

- 12 ounces pretrimmed haricots verts or thin green beans, cut into thirds
- 1 small lemon, zested and cut into 4 wedges
- 2 tablespoons pine nuts
- 1 8-ounce package precooked brown rice
- 2 tablespoons water
- Chopped fresh parsley for garnish

Directions:

1. Preheat oven to 425 degrees F. Line a rimmed baking sheet with foil or parchment paper.

2. Brush salmon with 1 tablespoon oil and place on the prepared baking sheet. Mash garlic and salt into a paste with the side of a chef's knife or a

fork. Combine a scant 1 teaspoon of the garlic paste in a small bowl with mayonnaise, mustard and 1/4 teaspoon pepper. Spread the mixture on top of the fish.

3. Roast the salmon until it flakes easily with a fork in the thickest part, 6 to 8 minutes per inch of thickness.

4. Meanwhile, heat the remaining 2 tablespoons oil in a large skillet over medium-high heat. Add green beans, lemon zest, pine nuts, the remaining garlic paste and 1/4 teaspoon pepper; cook, stirring, until the beans are just tender, 2 to 4 minutes. Reduce heat to medium. Add rice and water and cook, stirring, until hot, 2 to 3 minutes more.

5. Sprinkle the salmon with parsley, if desired, and serve with the green bean pilaf and lemon wedges.

Nutritional Value (Amount per Serving):

Calories: 541; Fat: 17.3; Carb: 56.58; Protein: 37.88

Instant Pot White Chicken Chili Freezer Pack

Prep Time: 15 Mins   Cook Time: 1 Hr   Serves: 8

Ingredients:

- 1 medium zucchini, chopped
- 1 ½ cups frozen corn kernels
- 1 large onion, chopped (about 1 1/3 cups)
- 3 cloves garlic, minced
- 2 tablespoons canned diced mild green chiles
- 1 tablespoon chili powder
- 1 ¾ teaspoons ground cumin
- 1 teaspoon dried oregano
- ½ teaspoon ground pepper
- ½ teaspoon salt
- 1 pound boneless, skinless chicken breast
- 1 ¾ cups dry great northern beans
- 4 cups low-sodium chicken broth
- 1 ½ cups water
- ⅓ cup chopped fresh cilantro, plus more for garnish
- 1 slice Lime wedges, sour cream and diced avocado

Directions:

1. To prep and freeze: Combine zucchini, corn, onion, garlic, chiles, chili powder, cumin, oregano, pepper and salt in a 64-ounce round, freezer-safe container. Layer the chicken on top, then the beans. Seal and freeze until ready to use, up to 3 months.

2. To cook: Let the frozen soup mix stand at room temperature for 10 minutes.

Invert the frozen soup mix into a multicooker (the beans should be at the bottom of the pot). Add broth and water. Lock lid in place and cook at high pressure for 30 minutes. Allow the pressure to release naturally.

3. Transfer the chicken to a cutting board and shred. Return the chicken to the pot and stir in cilantro. Serve topped with additional cilantro, lime wedges, sour cream and diced avocado, if desired.

Nutritional Value (Amount per Serving):

Calories: 308; Fat: 5.38; Carb: 48.47; Protein: 18.09

Stuffed Sweet Potato with Hummus Dressing

Prep Time: 15 Mins   Cook Time: 5 Mins   Serves: 1

Ingredients:
- 1 large sweet potato, scrubbed
- ¾ cup chopped kale
- 1 cup canned black beans, rinsed
- ¼ cup hummus
- 2 tablespoons water

Directions:

1. Prick sweet potato all over with a fork. Microwave on High until cooked through, 7 to 10 minutes.

2. Meanwhile, wash kale and drain, allowing water to cling to the leaves. Place in a medium saucepan; cover and cook over medium-high heat, stirring once or twice, until wilted. Add beans; add a tablespoon or two of water if the pot is dry. Continue cooking, uncovered, stirring occasionally, until the mixture is steaming hot, 1 to 2 minutes.

3. Split the sweet potato open and top with the kale and bean mixture. Combine hummus and 2 tablespoons water in a small dish. Add additional water as needed to reach desired consistency. Drizzle the hummus dressing over the stuffed sweet potato.

Nutritional Value (Amount per Serving):

Calories: 938; Fat: 8.42; Carb: 171.68; Protein: 49.02

Chapter 3: Dinner

Mashed Potatoes and Cauliflower with Sour Cream

Prep Time: 15 Mins   Cook Time: 20 Mins   Serves: 6

Ingredients:

- 12 ounces baking potatoes, peeled and cut into 1/2-inch cubes (about 2 1/2 cups)
- 1 1/4 pounds cauliflower, cut into 1-inch pieces (about 4 1/2 cups)
- 1/3 cup reduced-fat sour cream
- 1 tablespoon chives
- 1/2 teaspoon salt
- 1/4 teaspoon black pepper

Directions:

1. Combine cauliflower and potatoes in large saucepan; cover with water. Bring to a boil. Reduce heat; simmer about 10 to 12 minutes or until vegetables are tender. Drain.

2. Add sour cream, chives, salt, and pepper to saucepan. Using potato masher, mash until blended.

Nutritional Value (Amount per Serving):

Calories: 84; Fat: 0.36; Carb: 17.87; Protein: 3.54

Mediterranean Pork & Orzo

Prep Time: 10 Mins   Cook Time: 30 Mins   Serves: 6

Ingredients:

- 1-1/2 pounds pork tenderloin
- 1 teaspoon coarsely ground pepper
- 2 tablespoons olive oil
- 3 quarts water
- 1-1/4 cups uncooked orzo pasta
- 1/4 teaspoon salt
- 1 package (6 ounces) fresh baby spinach
- 1 cup grape tomatoes, halved
- 3/4 cup crumbled feta cheese

Directions:

1. Rub pork with pepper; cut into 1-in. cubes. In a large nonstick skillet, heat oil over medium heat. Add pork; cook and stir until no longer pink, 8-10 minutes.

2. Meanwhile, in a Dutch oven, bring water to a boil. Stir in orzo and salt; cook, uncovered, 8 minutes. Stir in spinach; cook until orzo is tender and spinach is wilted, 45-60 seconds longer. Drain.

3. Add tomatoes to pork; heat through. Stir in orzo mixture and cheese.

Calories: 249; Fat: 13.23; Carb: 11.14; Protein: 21.89

Cod and Asparagus Bake

Prep Time: 10 Mins   Cook Time: 15 Mins   Serves: 4

Ingredients:

- 4 cod fillets (6 ounces each)
- 1 teaspoon dried oregano
- 1/4 teaspoon salt
- 1 medium lemon, thinly sliced
- 1 shallot, thinly sliced
- 1/3 cup garlic-stuffed olives, halved
- 2 tablespoons water
- 2 tablespoons olive juice

Directions:

1. Place fillets in a large skillet coated with cooking spray. Sprinkle with oregano and salt; top with lemon and shallot.

2. Scatter olives around fish; add water and olive juice. Bring to a boil. Reduce heat to low; gently cook, covered, 8-10 minutes, or until fish just begins to flake easily with a fork.

Nutritional Value (Amount per Serving):

Calories: 107; Fat: 1.02; Carb: 5.39; Protein: 18.59

Mediterranean Chicken Pasta

Prep Time: 25 Mins   Cook Time: 20 Mins   Serves: 8

Ingredients:

- 1 package (12 ounces) uncooked tricolor spiral pasta
- 2 tablespoons olive oil, divided
- 1 pound boneless skinless chicken breasts, cut into 1/2-inch pieces
- 1 large sweet red pepper, chopped
- 1 medium onion, chopped
- 3 garlic cloves, peeled and thinly sliced
- 1 cup white wine or reduced-sodium chicken broth
- 1/4 cup julienned soft sun-dried tomatoes (not packed in oil)
- 1 teaspoon dried basil
- 1 teaspoon Italian seasoning
- 1/2 teaspoon salt
- 1/4 teaspoon crushed red pepper flakes
- 1/4 teaspoon pepper

- 1 can (14-1/2 ounces) reduced-sodium chicken broth
- 1 can (14 ounces) water-packed quartered artichoke hearts, drained
- 1 package (6 ounces) fresh baby spinach
- 1 cup (4 ounces) crumbled feta cheese
- Thinly sliced fresh basil leaves and shaved Parmesan cheese, optional

Directions:

1. Cook pasta according to package directions. In a 6-qt. stockpot, heat 1 tablespoon oil over medium-high heat. Add chicken; cook and stir 4-6 minutes or until no longer pink. Remove from pot.

2. In same pot, heat remaining oil over medium heat. Add red pepper and onion; cook and stir 4-5 minutes or until onion is tender. Add garlic; cook 1 minute longer. Add wine, sun-dried tomatoes and seasonings; bring to a boil. Reduce heat; simmer 5 minutes, stirring to loosen browned bits from pot.

3. Add broth and artichoke hearts; return to a boil. Stir in spinach and chicken; cook just until spinach is wilted.

4. Drain pasta; stir into chicken mixture. Stir in feta cheese. If desired, top servings with basil and Parmesan cheese.

Nutritional Value (Amount per Serving):

Calories: 218; Fat: 9.72; Carb: 14.25; Protein: 18.89

Green Bean and Red Pepper SautÉ

Prep Time: 10 Mins   Cook Time: 30 Mins   Serves: 6

Ingredients:

- 1 pound fresh green beans, ends trimmed
- 2 tablespoons olive oil
- 1 large red bell pepper, cut into strips
- 1 teaspoon lemon juice
- 1/4 cup chopped salted cashews
- Dash of black pepper

Directions:

1. In a large kettle, bring 3 quarts water to a boil. Add green beans and return water to a boil. Cook, uncovered, for 8 to 10 minutes until crisp-tender. Plunge beans into cold water to stop cooking. Beans may be covered and refrigerated overnight at this point. Heat oil in a large saucepan or wok until hot. Sauté red pepper over medium heat for 2 to 3 minutes. Stir

in beans, lemon juice, cashews, and pepper. Cook and stir gently until thoroughly heated, about 6 to 8 minutes. Transfer to a serving platter and serve immediately.

Nutritional Value (Amount per Serving):

Calories: 122; Fat: 10.52; Carb: 7.28; Protein: 2.29

Indian Summer Stew

Prep Time: 15 Mins   Cook Time: 50 Mins   Serves: 12

Ingredients:

- 6 new red potatoes (about 3/4 pound)
- 2 tablespoons olive oil
- 2 cloves garlic, minced
- 2 medium onions, chopped
- 1/2 teaspoon chili powder
- 1 teaspoon cumin
- 1 teaspoon thyme
- 1 teaspoon basil
- 1 teaspoon oregano
- 1 small eggplant, chopped into
- bite-size chunks
- 3 medium tomatoes, chopped
- 2 green bell peppers, sliced into strips
- 1/2 pound green beans, trimmed and cut into bite-size pieces
- 2 yellow squash, sliced
- 4 tablespoons tomato paste
- 2 cups corn
- 2 teaspoons caraway seeds
- 1/2 teaspoon black pepper

Directions:

1. In a medium saucepan, boil unpeeled potatoes in water until tender, about 15 minutes. Drain and set aside. In a large soup pot or kettle, heat oil over medium-high heat. Add garlic and sauté 1 minute. Add onions, chili powder, cumin, thyme, basil, and oregano. Stir. Add eggplant and tomatoes; simmer 10 minutes. Add pepper strips and green beans; simmer 10 minutes. Cut potatoes into bite-size pieces and add to pot. Add squash, tomato paste, corn, caraway seeds, and pepper. Stir well and cook over low heat for 10 to 15 more minutes until vegetables are tender but not mushy. Serve hot.

Nutritional Value (Amount per Serving):

Calories: 290; Fat: 4.23; Carb: 58.72; Protein: 7.8

Seared Salmon with Rose and Herb Pan Sauce

Prep Time: 19 Mins   Cook Time: 35 Mins   Serves: 12

Ingredients:

- 1½ cups rice, for serving
- 1 bunch trimmed asparagus, for serving
- 1 tbsp olive oil
- 2 6-oz portions skin-on wild salmon (center cut)
- Kosher salt and freshly ground pepper, to taste
- 1 lemon, halved
- 2 tbsp unsalted butter, divided
- 1 shallot, minced
- 1 tbsp fresh tarragon, chopped
- 1 tbsp fresh dill, chopped
- 1 tbsp fresh parsley, chopped
- 1 tbsp capers, rinsed
- ⅔ cup Bonterra rosé

Directions:

1. Cook the rice: Cook rice to desired doneness according to package instructions. Keep warm until ready to serve.

2. Roast the asparagus: Preheat oven to 400 degrees F.

3. Arrange asparagus on a baking sheet and drizzle with olive oil. Season with salt and pepper to taste. Roast until lightly caramelized and crisp-tender, about 18 to 20 minutes. Keep warm until ready to serve.

4. Prepare the salmon: Meanwhile, season salmon on both sides with salt and pepper and let sit at room temperature for about 10 minutes.

5. In a coated cast-iron skillet or heavy-bottomed frying pan, add the olive oil and heat over medium high heat until shimmering. Add salmon (skin side up) and halved lemon and cook for about 4 minutes, or until salmon is golden brown and can easily move around the pan. Remove lemon from the pan and set aside on a plate. Flip salmon and cook skin side down for another 3 minutes, then add to the plate with the lemon and tent loosely with foil.

6. Drain olive oil from the skillet and add 1 tbsp of butter. Once melted, add shallot and cook for about 2 minutes or until they start to soften. Deglaze the pan with the rosé, scraping up brown bits from the bottom of the pan. Bring wine to a boil, then reduce heat and simmer until the liquid has reduced by half. Season with salt and pepper, then remove from heat.

7. Add the capers, herbs, and remaining 1 tbsp of butter, and mount the sauce by slowly swirling the butter around in the pan.

8. Serve the salmon on top of prepared rice with roasted asparagus and a spoonful of the rosé pan sauce.

Nutritional Value (Amount per Serving):

Calories: 251; Fat: 11.32; Carb: 29.45; Protein: 13.13

Cauliflower Pilaf

Prep Time: 10 Mins   Cook Time: 10 Mins   Serves: 4

Ingredients:

- 1 large head cauliflower, cut into florets
- 2 tablespoons extra-virgin olive oil
- Pinch asafetida
- 1/2 cup vegetable stock
- Sea salt
- 1/2 cup golden raisins
- 1/2 cup slivered almonds
- 1/4 cup chopped fresh flat-leaf Italian parsley

Directions:

1. In a food processor fitted with the metal blade, process the cauliflower florets until they resemble the texture of rice (you can also grate them on the large holes of a box grater). Set aside.

2. In a medium skillet over medium-high heat, heat the olive oil. Add the asafetida and cook for about 45 seconds, stirring constantly until fragrant.

3. Add the cauliflower and cook for 2 to 3 minutes, stirring constantly until it softens slightly.

4. Stir in the vegetable stock and season to taste. Reduce the heat to low, cover and cook for 5 more minutes until the cauliflower is tender.

5. Remove from the heat and gently fold in the raisins, almonds and parsley. Taste and adjust the seasonings. Serve.

Nutritional Value (Amount per Serving):

Calories: 345; Fat: 30.66; Carb: 20.14; Protein: 23.8

Cauliflower Potato Pancakes

Prep Time: 10 Mins   Cook Time: 15 Mins   Serves: 6

Ingredients:

- 1 1/2 cups cubed Yukon Gold potatoes
- 3 cups roughly chopped cauliflower
- 1/3 cup whole wheat flour
- 1 egg, lightly beaten
- 1 egg white

- 1 tablespoon chopped fresh chives, plus additional for garnish
- 1 teaspoon baking powder
- 1/2 teaspoon salt
- 3 teaspoons vegetable oil, divided
- Light sour cream (optional)

Directions:

1. Bring large saucepan of water to a boil. Add potatoes and cauliflower; reduce heat. Simmer 10 minutes or until fork-tender. Drain potatoes and cauliflower. Let stand 5 to 10 minutes or until cool enough to handle.

2. Gently mash potatoes and cauliflower in large bowl. Add flour, egg, egg white, 1 tablespoon chives, baking powder, and salt; mix well.

3. Heat 1 teaspoon oil in large nonstick skillet over medium heat. Drop 1/4 cupfuls potato mixture into skillet; flatten slightly. Cook 5 to 7 minutes per side or until golden brown. Repeat with remaining oil and potato mixture.

4. Serve with sour cream, if desired. Garnish with additional chives.

Nutritional Value (Amount per Serving):

Calories: 113; Fat: 4.6; Carb: 14.65; Protein: 4.82

Mediterranean Chicken

Prep Time: 10 Mins   Cook Time: 15 Mins   Serves: 4

Ingredients:

- 4 boneless skinless chicken breast halves (6 ounces each)
- 1/4 teaspoon salt
- 1/4 teaspoon pepper
- 3 tablespoons olive oil
- 1 pint grape tomatoes
- 16 pitted Greek or ripe olives, sliced
- 3 tablespoons capers, drained

Directions:

1. Sprinkle chicken with salt and pepper. In a large ovenproof skillet, cook chicken in oil over medium heat until golden brown, 2-3 minutes on each side. Add the tomatoes, olives and capers.

2. Bake, uncovered, at 475°F until a thermometer reads 165°F, 10-14 minutes.

Nutritional Value (Amount per Serving):

Calories: 392; Fat: 18.03; Carb: 1.22; Protein: 53.43

Feta Shrimp Skillet

Prep Time: 10 Mins   Cook Time: 20 Mins   Serves: 4

Ingredients:

- 1 tablespoon olive oil
- 1 medium onion, finely chopped
- 3 garlic cloves, minced
- 1 teaspoon dried oregano
- 1/2 teaspoon pepper
- 1/4 teaspoon salt
- 2 cans (14-1/2 ounces each) diced tomatoes, undrained
- 1/4 cup white wine, optional
- 1 pound uncooked shrimp (31-40 per pound), peeled and deveined
- 2 tablespoons minced fresh parsley
- 3/4 cup crumbled feta cheese

Directions:

1. In a large nonstick skillet, heat oil over medium-high heat. Add onion; cook and stir 4-6 minutes or until tender. Add garlic and seasonings; cook 1 minute longer. Stir in tomatoes and, if desired, wine. Bring to a boil. Reduce heat; simmer, uncovered, 5-7 minutes or until sauce is slightly thickened.

2. Add shrimps and parsley; cook 5-6 minutes or until shrimps turn pink, stirring occasionally. Remove from heat; sprinkle with cheese. Let stand, covered, until cheese is softened.

Nutritional Value (Amount per Serving):

Calories: 252; Fat: 11.22; Carb: 8.74; Protein: 28.61

Creamy Pesto Spaghetti Squash

Prep Time: 10 Mins   Cook Time: 20 Mins   Serves: 4

Ingredients:

- 1 (2 1/2 to 3-pound) cooked, halved spaghetti squash
- 1 pint cherry tomatoes
- 1 bunch fresh basil
- 1 cup basil pesto
- 1/2 cup heavy cream
- 1 teaspoon kosher salt
- Grated Parmesan cheese (optional)

Directions:

1. Scrape the strands from a cooked spaghetti squash out with a fork. Halve 1 pint cherry tomatoes. Pick the leaves from 1 bunch fresh basil, then thinly slice the leaves (about 1 1/4 cups).

2. Bring 1 cup basil pesto and 1/2 cup heavy cream to a simmer in a large skillet or saucepan over medium heat. Add the spaghetti squash strands, tomatoes, and 1 teaspoon kosher salt. Stir to coat in the creamy pesto and cook until warmed through, 4 to 5 minutes. Reserve a small amount of the basil for garnish, then stir the remaining into the spaghetti squash. Garnish with the reserved basil and and serve with grated Parmesan cheese if desired.

Nutritional Value (Amount per Serving):

Calories: 68; Fat: 6.03; Carb: 2.74; Protein: 1.49

Lemony Roasted Shrimp and Asparagus

Prep Time: 10-15 Mins   Cook Time: 8-10 Mins   Serves: 4

Ingredients:

- 1 (16-ounce) bag Trader Joe's Raw Wild Argentinian Red Shrimp
- 1 (12-ounce) bag Trader Joe's frozen Asparagus Spears
- (Regular or Grilled)
- Kosher salt
- Freshly ground black pepper
- 2 medium lemons

Directions:

1. Arrange a rack in the middle of the oven and heat the oven to 400°F. Meanwhile, empty 1 (16-ounce) bag Raw Wild Argentinian Red Shrimp into a colander in the sink, and run cool water over the shrimps, tossing occasionally, until defrosted, 5 to 10 minutes. Pat dry and place on a rimmed baking sheet.

2. Empty 1 (12-ounce) bag frozen Asparagus Spears (Grilled or Regular) onto the baking sheet. Drizzle with 2 tablespoons olive oil, season with kosher salt and black pepper, toss to coat, and spread out in an even layer.

3. Thinly slice 1 medium lemon, remove any seeds, and tuck the slices under the shrimps and asparagus. Roast, stirring halfway through, until the shrimps are pink and opaque, 8 to 10 minutes total.

4. Halve another 1 medium lemon crosswise, squeeze the juice over the shrimps and asparagus, and serve.

Nutritional Value (Amount per Serving):

Calories: 396; Fat: 16.93; Carb: 34.16; Protein: 27.93

Dill Pickle Chicken

Prep Time: 10 Mins   Cook Time: 20 Mins   Serves: 4

Ingredients:

- 2 pounds boneless, skinless chicken thighs (4 to 6 thighs)
- 2 cups pickle brine (from a 32-ounce jar or larger)
- Kosher salt
- Freshly ground black pepper
- 1/2 cup diced pickles (about 2 pickles, optional)
- 2 tablespoons chopped fresh dill (optional)

Directions:

1. Place the chicken in a shallow dish or container, and pour the brine over the top. If necessary, rearrange the chicken so each piece is completely submerged. Cover and refrigerate for 2 to 8 hours.

2. Arrange a rack in the middle of the oven and heat to 425°F. Drain the chicken and pat dry with paper towels. Liberally season the chicken with salt and pepper on both sides. Place the chicken thighs in a single layer in an 8- or 9-inch square baking dish.

3. Roast until the chicken reaches an internal temperature of 165°F, about 20 minutes. Cover with aluminum foil, and let the chicken rest for 10 minutes. Garnish with chopped pickles and fresh dill, and serve warm.

Nutritional Value (Amount per Serving):

Calories: 648; Fat: 29.91; Carb: 51.35; Protein: 42.1

Greek Lamb Burgers

Prep Time: 10 Mins   Cook Time: 10 Mins   Serves: 4

Ingredients:

- 1 pound lean ground lamb
- 2 tablespoons red onion, finely chopped
- 1/2 cup cilantro, chopped
- 2 tablespoons fat-free feta cheese
- 1/2 teaspoon cumin
- 1/8 teaspoon cayenne pepper
- 1/4 teaspoon salt
- 1/4 teaspoon black pepper

Directions:

1. Preheat grill to medium-high. In a large bowl, gently mix all ingredients until combined. Form into 4 burgers.

2. Grill for about 4 to 5 minutes on each side, or until desired doneness.

Nutritional Value (Amount per Serving):

Calories: 303; Fat: 23.67; Carb: 1.52; Protein: 21.02

Mediterranean Grilled Lamb Chops

Prep Time: 10 Mins   Cook Time: 10 Mins   Serves: 4

Ingredients:

- 1 (1-pound) eggplant, peeled and sliced into 1/4-inch slices
- 1 red onion, sliced into 1/4-inch slices
- Cooking spray
- 1 tablespoon olive oil
- 3 tablespoons lemon juice
- 2 tablespoons chopped fresh mint
- 1/4 cup chopped fresh parsley
- 1 teaspoon salt
- 1/8 teaspoon cayenne pepper
- 1/4 teaspoon black pepper
- 1 1/2 pound loin lamb chops, (about 8) well-trimmed

Directions:

1. Preheat grill to medium-high.

2. Coat both sides of eggplant and onion slices with cooking spray. Grill vegetables 2 to 3 minutes, turning once, until browned on both sides. Transfer to a cutting board and let cool slightly. Chop and combine in a medium bowl with oil, lemon juice, mint, parsley, 1/2 teaspoon salt, and cayenne. Set aside.

3. Meanwhile, sprinkle lamb with black pepper and the reamining salt. Grill chops about 4 minutes per side, or until browned on both sides and cooked to desired doneness. Serve with eggplant salad.

Nutritional Value (Amount per Serving):

Calories: 479; Fat: 24.11; Carb: 10.22; Protein: 55.79

Lemon Dijon Lamb Chops

Prep Time: 10 Mins   Cook Time: 12 Mins   Serves: 4

Ingredients:

- 1/8 teaspoon salt
- 1/2 teaspoon black pepepr
- 1/4 teaspoon dried thyme
- 2 cloves garlic, minced
- 2 teaspoons Dijon mustard
- 2 teaspoons lemon juice

- 1 teaspoon olive oil
- 4 (5-ounce) lean lamb loin chops, well-trimmed

Directions:

1. Preheat the broiler. In a small bowl, combine salt, pepper, thyme, and garlic. Stir in mustard, lemon juice, and olive oil.

2. Spread mixture over both sides of chops. Place chops on a lightly greased rack in a broiler pan.

3. Broil 6 to 7 minutes on each side or to desired degree of doneness.

Nutritional Value (Amount per Serving):

Calories: 74; Fat: 4.11; Carb: 0.88; Protein: 8.6

Garlicky Mustard Lamb Chops

Prep Time: 10 Mins   Cook Time: 14 Mins   Serves: 4

Ingredients:

- 4 cloves, garlic, minced
- 1 teaspoon Dijon mustard
- 1/2 teaspoon pepper
- 1/4 teaspoon dried thyme
- 1/8 teaspoon salt
- 1 teaspoon chopped fresh parsely
- 2 teaspoons lemon juice
- 1 tablespoon olive oil
- 4 (5-ounce) lean lamb loin chops

Directions:

1. Preheat the broiler. In a small bowl, combine all ingredients except lamb chops; mix well.

2. Trim fat from lamb chops. Spread garlic mixture over both sides of chops. Place chops on a lightly greased rack in a broiler pan. Broil 6 to 7 minutes on each side or to desired degree of doneness.

Nutritional Value (Amount per Serving):

Calories: 180; Fat: 10.68; Carb: 1.78; Protein: 18.81

Foil-Packet Lamb Chops

Prep Time: 10 Mins   Cook Time: 45 Mins   Serves: 6

Ingredients:

- 1/2 teaspoon salt
- 1/4 teaspoon black pepper
- 1 tablespoon all-purpose flour
- 12 (2-ounce) lamb rib chops
- 1 (1-ounce) package dry onion soup mix
- 1 red bell pepper, thinly sliced
- 1 (8-ounce) package sliced fresh mushrooms
- 1/2 (14-ounce) can reduced-sodium diced tomatoes, undrained
- 1 tablespoon steak sauce

Directions:

1. Preheat oven to 375 degrees F. In a small bowl, combine salt, pepper, and flour.

2. Tear off 1 (18- x 28-inch) piece heavy-duty aluminum foil. Place foil in a 9- x 13-inch baking dish.

3. Place chops in pan; sprinkle evenly with flour mixture. Top with soup mix and remaining ingredients.

4. Bring up 2 long sides of foil sheet; fold together, an then fold again. Repeat with short ends, forming a packet and leaving room for heat to circulate inside packet.

5. Bake for 45 minutes or until cooked through. Carefully open packets, as steam will escape.

Nutritional Value (Amount per Serving):

Calories: 295; Fat: 13.77; Carb: 3.71; Protein: 36.55

Mediterranean Lamb Meatballs

Prep Time: 10 Mins   Cook Time: 10 Mins   Serves: 5

Ingredients:

- 15 (6- to 8-inch) wooden or metal skewers
- 1 1/4 pound lean ground lamb
- 2 tablespoons tomato sauce
- 1/4 cup chopped fresh parlsey
- 1/2 onion, finely chopped (about 1/2 cup)
- 1/2 teaspoon oregano
- 1/2 teaspoon salt
- 1/4 teaspoon black pepper

Directions:

1. If using wooden skewers, soak in water 15 to 20 minutes. Preheat broiler.

2. In a large bowl, combine all ingredients; mix well. Roll mixture into 15 balls and place on a rimmed baking sheet or broiler pan.

3. Place one skewer into the end of each lamb meatball and broil 5 to 7 minutes on each side, turning once, until cooked through.

Nutritional Value (Amount per Serving):

Calories: 1288; Fat: 83.07; Carb: 4.09; Protein: 131.27

Greek Festival Fish

Prep Time: 10 Mins   Cook Time: 20 Mins   Serves: 6

Ingredients:

- 2 tablespoons olive oil
- 8 scallions, thinly sliced
- 2 cloves garlic, minced
- 4 tomatoes, chopped
- 1/2 cup dry white wine
- 2 tablespoons finely chopped parsley
- 1 teaspoon dried oregano
- 1 teaspoon black pepper
- 6 white-fleshed fish fillets (2 pounds total) such as tilapia, flounder, or sole
- 1 (4-ounce) package crumbled feta cheese

Directions:

1. Preheat the oven to 400 degrees. Coat a 9-inch by 13-inch baking dish with cooking spray.

2. In a medium skillet, heat the oil over medium heat. Add the scallions and garlic and sauté until tender. Add the tomatoes, wine, parsley, oregano, and pepper. Simmer for 5 minutes, or until the sauce thickens. Remove from the heat.

3. Place half of the sauce mixture in the baking dish. Arrange the fish fillets over the sauce and cover with the remaining sauce. Sprinkle with the feta cheese.

4. Bake for 15 to 18 minutes, or until the fish flakes easily with a fork. Serve immediately.

Nutritional Value (Amount per Serving):

Calories: 568; Fat: 35.62; Carb: 37.84; Protein: 25.7

Tropical Chicken Cauliflower Rice Bowls

Prep Time: 40 Mins   Cook Time: 10 Mins   Serves: 4

Ingredients:

- 1 fresh pineapple, peeled, cored and cubed (about 3 cups), divided
- 1/2 cup plain or coconut Greek yogurt
- 2 tablespoons plus 1/2 cup chopped fresh cilantro, divided
- 3 tablespoons lime juice, divided
- 3/4 teaspoon salt, divided
- 1/4 teaspoon crushed red pepper flakes
- 1/8 teaspoon chili powder
- 4 boneless skinless chicken breast halves (6 ounces each)
- 3 cups fresh cauliflower florets (about 1/2 small cauliflower)
- 1 tablespoon canola oil
- 1 small red onion, finely chopped
- Optional: Toasted sweetened shredded coconut or lime wedges

Directions:

1. For marinade, place 1 cup pineapple, yogurt, 2 tablespoons each of cilantro and lime juice, 1/4 teaspoon salt, pepper flakes and chili powder in a food processor; process until blended. In a large bowl, toss chicken with marinade; refrigerate, covered, 1-3 hours.

2. In a clean food processor, pulse cauliflower until it resembles rice (do not overprocess). In a large skillet, heat oil over medium-high heat; saute onion until lightly browned, 3-5 minutes. Add cauliflower; cook and stir until lightly browned, 5-7 minutes. Stir in 1 cup pineapple and the remaining 1 tablespoon lime juice and 1/2 teaspoon salt; cook, covered, over medium heat until cauliflower is tender, 3-5 minutes. Stir in remaining 1/2 cup cilantro. Keep warm.

3. Preheat grill or broiler. Drain chicken, discarding marinade. Place chicken on an oiled grill rack over medium heat or in a greased foil-lined 15x10x1-in. pan. Grill, covered, or broil 4 in. from heat until a thermometer reads 165°F, 4-6 minutes per side. Let stand 5 minutes before slicing.

4. To serve, divide cauliflower mixture between 4 bowls. Top with chicken, remaining 1 cup pineapple and, if desired, coconut and lime wedges.

Nutritional Value (Amount per Serving):

Calories: 527; Fat: 18.43; Carb: 32.02; Protein: 58.59

Slow-Cooker Pork Chops

Prep Time: 15 Mins   Cook Time: 2 Hrs   Serves: 4

Ingredients:

- 1/2 cup all-purpose flour, divided
- 1/2 teaspoon ground mustard
- 1/2 teaspoon garlic pepper blend
- 1/4 teaspoon seasoned salt
- 4 boneless pork loin chops (4 ounces each)
- 2 tablespoons canola oil
- 1 can (14-1/2 ounces) chicken broth

Directions:

1. In a shallow bowl, combine 1/4 cup flour, mustard, garlic pepper and seasoned salt. Add pork chops, one at a time, and dredge to coat. In a large skillet, brown chops in oil on both sides.

2. Transfer to a 5-qt. slow cooker. Pour broth over chops. Cook, covered, on low for 2-3 hours or until meat is tender.

3. Remove pork to a serving plate and keep warm. Whisk remaining flour into cooking juices until smooth; cook, covered, on high until gravy is thickened.

Nutritional Value (Amount per Serving):

Calories: 416; Fat: 16.4; Carb: 12.53; Protein: 50.98

Sweet & Tangy Salmon with Green Beans

Prep Time: 20 Mins   Cook Time: 15 Mins   Serves: 4

Ingredients:

- 4 salmon fillets (6 ounces each)
- 1 tablespoon butter
- 2 tablespoons brown sugar
- 2 tablespoons reduced-sodium soy sauce
- 2 tablespoons Dijon mustard
- 1 tablespoon olive oil
- 1/2 teaspoon pepper
- 1/8 teaspoon salt
- 1 pound fresh green beans, trimmed

Directions:

1. Preheat oven to 425°F. Place fillets in a 15x10x1-in. baking pan coated with cooking spray. In a small skillet, melt butter; stir in brown sugar, soy sauce, mustard, oil, pepper and salt. Brush half of the mixture over salmon.

2. Place green beans in a large bowl; drizzle with remaining brown sugar mixture and toss to coat. Arrange green beans around fillets. Roast until fish just begins to flake easily with a fork and green beans are crisp-tender, 14-16 minutes.

Nutritional Value (Amount per Serving):

Calories: 735; Fat: 36.97; Carb: 7.75; Protein: 88.37

Parmesan Chicken with Artichoke Hearts

Prep Time: 20 Mins   Cook Time: 20 Mins   Serves: 4

Ingredients:

- 4 boneless skinless chicken breast halves (6 ounces each)
- 3 teaspoons olive oil, divided
- 1 teaspoon dried rosemary, crushed
- 1/2 teaspoon dried thyme
- 1/2 teaspoon pepper
- 2 cans (14 ounces each) water-packed artichoke hearts, drained and quartered
- 1 medium onion, coarsely chopped
- 1/2 cup white wine or reduced-sodium chicken broth
- 2 garlic cloves, chopped
- 1/4 cup shredded Parmesan cheese
- 1 lemon, cut into 8 slices
- 2 green onions, thinly sliced

Directions:

1. Preheat oven to 375°F. Place chicken in a 15x10x1-in. baking pan coated with cooking spray; drizzle with 1-1/2 teaspoons oil. In a small bowl, mix rosemary, thyme and pepper; sprinkle half over chicken.

2. In a large bowl, combine artichoke hearts, onion, wine, garlic, remaining oil and remaining herb mixture; toss to coat. Arrange around chicken. Sprinkle chicken with cheese; top with lemon slices.

3. Roast until a thermometer inserted in chicken reads 165°, 20-25 minutes. Sprinkle with green onions.

Nutritional Value (Amount per Serving):

Calories: 496; Fat: 19.55; Carb: 22.1; Protein: 58.94

Greek-Style Chicken Pittas

Prep Time: 15 Mins   Cook Time: 5 Mins   Serves: 2

Ingredients:

- 250g chicken breast, sliced into strips
- 1 tsp dried oregano
- Juice half lemon
- 3 cloves garlic, crushed
- good grind black pepper
- 50g cucumber, finely diced
- 60g 0% fat Greek-style yogurt
- 2 fresh tomatoes, sliced
- 10 fresh mint leaves, torn
- 80g salad leaves
- 2 tsp olive oil

- 2 wholemeal pittas
- lemon wedges, to serve

Directions:

1. Mix the chicken strips, oregano, lemon juice, garlic and black pepper together and set aside to infuse for 10 minutes.

2. Meanwhile, in a bowl mix together the cucumber and yogurt. Add tomatoes and mint together and mix with the salad leaves.

3. Heat the oil in a small pan, add the chicken and mix well to ensure even cooking – it should take around 4 minutes.

4. Warm the pitta bread in a dry frying pan or toaster and cut in half and open to create pockets. Fill with salad and chicken, squeeze with lemon juice from the wedges and drizzle with the yogurt and cucumber mix.

Nutritional Value (Amount per Serving):

Calories: 662; Fat: 47.95; Carb: 22.23; Protein: 40.39

Slow-Cooker Chicken & Orzo with Tomatoes & Olives

Prep Time: 15 Mins   Cook Time: 2 Hrs 15 Mins   Serves: 4

Ingredients:

- 1 pound boneless, skinless chicken breasts, trimmed
- 1 cup low-sodium chicken broth
- 2 medium tomatoes, chopped
- 1 medium onion, halved and sliced
- Zest and juice of 1 lemon
- 1 teaspoon herbes de Provence
- ½ teaspoon salt
- ½ teaspoon ground pepper
- ¾ cup whole-wheat orzo
- ⅓ cup quartered black or green olives
- 2 tablespoons chopped fresh parsley

Directions:

1. Cut each chicken breast half into 4 pieces. Combine the chicken, broth, tomatoes, onion, lemon zest, lemon juice, herbes de Provence, salt and pepper in a 6-quart slow cooker. Cook on High for 1 hour, 30 minutes or on Low for 3 hours, 30 minutes. Stir in orzo and olives; cover and cook until the orzo is tender, about 30 minutes more. Let cool slightly. Sprinkle with parsley before serving.

Nutritional Value (Amount per Serving):

Calories: 257; Fat: 7.17; Carb: 35.47; Protein: 13.89

Chickpea Pasta with Lemony-Parsley Pesto

Prep Time: 20 Mins   Cook Time: 10 Mins   Serves: 2

Ingredients:

- 4 ounces chickpea penne or other penne pasta (about 1 1/4 cups dry)
- 1 bunch flat-leaf parsley (about 4 cups lightly packed), plus more for garnish
- 3 cloves garlic
- ⅓ cup extra-virgin olive oil
- 1 teaspoon lemon zest
- 2 tablespoons lemon juice
- ½ teaspoon kosher salt
- ¼ teaspoon ground black pepper
- 1 1/2 cups roasted root vegetables (see associated recipe)

Directions:

1. Cook pasta according to package directions. Drain well.

2. Meanwhile, combine parsley and garlic in a food processor and pulse until uniformly chopped, about 10 times. Add oil, lemon juice, salt and pepper and puree until just combined, about 15 seconds; it should be chunky.

3. Microwave roasted root vegetables in a microwave-safe bowl until heated through, about 1 minute. (Alternatively, heat 1 teaspoon extra-virgin olive oil in a large skillet over medium-high heat. Add vegetables and cook, stirring often, until heated through, 2 to 4 minutes.)

4. Toss the hot pasta with the pesto, the vegetables and lemon zest. Garnish with parsley, if desired.

Nutritional Value (Amount per Serving):

Calories: 431; Fat: 18.34; Carb: 61.04; Protein: 89.2

Caprese Stuffed Portobello Mushrooms

Prep Time: 25 Mins   Cook Time: 15 Mins   Serves: 4

Ingredients:

- 3 tablespoons extra-virgin olive oil, divided
- 1 medium clove garlic, minced
- ½ teaspoon salt, divided
- ½ teaspoon ground pepper, divided
- 4 portobello mushrooms (about 14 ounces), stems and gills removed (see Tip)
- 1 cup halved cherry tomatoes
- ½ cup fresh mozzarella pearls, drained and patted dry
- ½ cup thinly sliced fresh basil

- 2 teaspoons best-quality balsamic vinegar

Directions:

1. Preheat oven to 400 degrees F.

2. Combine 2 tablespoons oil, garlic, 1/4 teaspoon salt and 1/4 teaspoon pepper in a small bowl. Using a silicone brush, coat mushrooms all over with the oil mixture. Place on a large rimmed baking sheet and bake until the mushrooms are mostly soft, about 10 minutes.

3. Meanwhile, stir tomatoes, mozzarella, basil and the remaining 1/4 teaspoon salt, 1/4 teaspoon pepper and 1 tablespoon oil together in a medium bowl. Once the mushrooms have softened, remove from the oven and fill with the tomato mixture. Bake until the cheese is fully melted and the tomatoes have wilted, about 12 to 15 minutes more. Drizzle each mushroom with 1/2 teaspoon vinegar and serve.

Nutritional Value (Amount per Serving):

Calories: 129; Fat: 7.15; Carb: 13.59; Protein: 5.45

Herby Cod with Roasted Tomatoes

Prep Time: 5 Mins   Cook Time: 10 Mins   Serves: 4

Ingredients:

- 4 (4 ounce) fresh or frozen skinless cod fillets, 3/4- to 1-inch thick
- 2 teaspoons snipped fresh oregano
- 1 teaspoon snipped fresh thyme
- ½ teaspoon salt
- ¼ teaspoon garlic powder
- ¼ teaspoon paprika
- ¼ teaspoon black pepper

- Nonstick cooking spray
- 3 cups cherry tomatoes
- 2 cloves garlic, sliced
- 1 tablespoon olive oil
- 2 tablespoons sliced pitted ripe olives
- 2 teaspoons capers
- Fresh oregano and/or thyme leaves

Directions:

1. Preheat oven to 450 degrees F. Thaw fish, if frozen. Rinse fish and pat dry with paper towels. In a small bowl combine snipped oregano, snipped thyme, salt, garlic powder, paprika and black pepper. Sprinkle half of the oregano mixture over both sides of each fish fillet.

2. Line a 15x10x1-inch baking pan with foil. Coat foil with cooking spray. Place fish on one side of the foil-lined pan. Add tomatoes and garlic slices to the other side of the foil-lined pan. Combine remaining oregano mixture with oil. Drizzle oil mixture over tomatoes; toss to coat. Bake for 8 to 12 minutes or until fish flakes easily when tested with a fork, stirring tomato mixture once. Stir olives and capers into cooked tomato mixture.

3. Divide fish and roasted tomato mixture evenly among four serving plates. Garnish with fresh oregano and/or thyme leaves.

Nutritional Value (Amount per Serving):

Calories: 276; Fat: 10.42; Carb: 42.63; Protein: 6.18

Slow-Cooker Pasta E Fagioli Soup Freezer Pack

Prep Time: 15 Mins   Cook Time: 8 Hrs   Serves: 6

Ingredients:

- 2 cups chopped onions
- 1 cup chopped carrots
- 1 cup chopped celery
- 1 pound cooked Meal-Prep Sheet-Pan Chicken Thighs (see associated recipe), diced
- 4 cups cooked whole-wheat rotini pasta
- 6 cups reduced-sodium chicken broth
- 4 teaspoons dried Italian seasoning
- ¼ teaspoon salt
- 1 (15 ounce) can no-salt-added white beans, rinsed
- 4 cups baby spinach (half of a 5-ounce box)
- 4 tablespoons chopped fresh basil, divided (Optional)
- 2 tablespoons best-quality extra-virgin olive oil
- ½ cup grated Parmigiano-Reggiano cheese

Directions:

1. Place onions, carrots and celery in a large sealable plastic bag. Place cooled cooked chicken and cooked pasta together in another bag. Seal both bags and freeze for up to 5 days. Defrost the bags in the refrigerator overnight before proceeding.

2. Transfer the vegetable mixture to a large slow cooker. Add broth, Italian seasoning and salt. Cover and cook on Low for 7 1/4 hours.

3. Add beans, spinach, 2 tablespoons basil, if using, and the defrosted chicken and pasta. Cook for 45 minutes more. Ladle the soup into bowls. Drizzle a little oil into each bowl and top with cheese and the remaining 2

tablespoons basil, if desired.

Nutritional Value (Amount per Serving):

Calories: 597; Fat: 30.22; Carb: 52.07; Protein: 33.04

One-Pot Spinach, Chicken Sausage & Feta Pasta

Prep Time: 20 Mins   Cook Time: 20 Mins   Serves: 4

Ingredients:

- 2 tablespoons olive oil
- 3 links cooked chicken sausage (9 ounces), sliced into rounds
- 1 cup diced onion (see Tip)
- 1 clove garlic, minced
- 1 (8 ounce) can no-salt-added tomato sauce
- 4 cups lightly packed baby spinach (half of a 5-ounce box)
- 6 cups cooked whole-wheat rotini pasta
- ¼ cup chopped pitted Kalamata olives
- ½ cup finely crumbled feta cheese
- ¼ cup chopped fresh basil (Optional)

Directions:

1. Heat oil in a large straight-sided skillet over medium-high heat. Add sausage, onion and garlic; cook, stirring often, until the onion is starting to brown, 4 to 6 minutes. Add tomato sauce, spinach, pasta and olives; cook, stirring often, until bubbling hot and the spinach is wilted, 3 to 5 minutes. Add 1 to 2 tablespoons water, if necessary, to keep the pasta from sticking. Stir in feta and basil, if using.

Nutritional Value (Amount per Serving):

Calories: 1076; Fat: 63.66; Carb: 80.46; Protein: 49.38

Chickpea & Quinoa Bowl with Roasted Red Pepper Sauce

Prep Time: 20 Mins   Cook Time: 20 Mins   Serves: 4

Ingredients:

- 1 (7 ounce) jar roasted red peppers, rinsed
- ¼ cup slivered almonds
- 4 tablespoons extra-virgin olive oil, divided
- 1 small clove garlic, minced
- 1 teaspoon paprika
- ½ teaspoon ground cumin
- ¼ teaspoon crushed red pepper (optional)

- 2 cups cooked quinoa
- ¼ cup Kalamata olives, chopped
- ¼ cup finely chopped red onion
- 1 (15 ounce) can chickpeas, rinsed
- 1 cup diced cucumber
- ¼ cup crumbled feta cheese
- 2 tablespoons finely chopped fresh parsley

Directions:

1. Place peppers, almonds, 2 tablespoons oil, garlic, paprika, cumin and crushed red pepper (if using) in a mini food processor. Puree until fairly smooth.

2. Combine quinoa, olives, red onion and the remaining 2 tablespoons oil in a medium bowl.

3. To serve, divide the quinoa mixture among 4 bowls and top with equal amounts of the chickpeas, cucumber and the red pepper sauce. Sprinkle with feta and parsley.

Nutritional Value (Amount per Serving):

Calories: 316; Fat: 13.04; Carb: 40.26; Protein: 10.99

Chapter 4: Vegetables

Turkey-Stuffed Bell Peppers

Prep Time: 30 Mins   Cook Time: 20 Mins   Serves: 5

Ingredients:

- 5 medium green, red or yellow peppers
- 2 teaspoons olive oil
- 1-1/4 pounds extra-lean ground turkey (99% lean)
- 1 large onion, chopped
- 1 garlic clove, minced
- 2 teaspoons ground cumin
- 1 teaspoon Italian seasoning
- 1/2 teaspoon salt
- 1/2 teaspoon pepper
- 2 medium tomatoes, finely chopped
- 1-3/4 cups shredded cheddar-flavored lactose-free or other cheese
- 1-1/2 cups soft bread crumbs
- 1/4 teaspoon paprika

Directions:

1. Preheat oven to 325°F. Cut peppers lengthwise in half; remove seeds. Place in a 15x10x1-in. pan coated with cooking spray.

2. In a large skillet, heat oil over medium-high heat. Cook and crumble turkey with onion, garlic and seasonings over medium-high heat until meat is no longer pink, 6-8 minutes. Cool slightly. Stir in tomatoes, cheese and bread crumbs.

3. Fill pepper halves with turkey mixture. Sprinkle with paprika. Bake, uncovered, until filling is heated through and peppers are tender, 20-25 minutes.

Nutritional Value (Amount per Serving):

Calories: 186; Fat: 4.74; Carb: 17.36; Protein: 20.53

Salmon & Spinach Salad with Avocado

Prep Time: 10 Mins   Cook Time: 10 Mins   Serves: 2

Ingredients:

- 1 salmon fillet (6 ounces)
- 2 tablespoons balsamic vinaigrette, divided
- 3 cups fresh baby spinach
- 1/4 cup cubed avocado
- 1 tablespoon chopped walnuts, toasted
- 1 tablespoon sunflower kernels, toasted
- 1 tablespoon dried cranberries

Directions:

1. Drizzle salmon with 1 tablespoon vinaigrette. Place on a broiler pan coated with cooking spray. Broil 3-4 in. from the heat for 10-15 minutes or until fish flakes easily with a fork. Cut salmon into 2 pieces.

2. Meanwhile, in a large bowl, toss spinach with remaining vinaigrette. Divide between 2 plates. Top with the salmon, avocado, walnuts, sunflower kernels and cranberries.

Nutritional Value (Amount per Serving):

Calories: 435; Fat: 22.67; Carb: 10.14; Protein: 47.77

Speedy Mediterranean Gnocchi

Prep Time: 5 Mins   Cook Time: 5 Mins   Serves: 2

Ingredients:

- 400g gnocchi
- 200g chargrilled vegetables (from the deli counter - I used chargrilled peppers, aubergines, artichokes and semi-dried tomatoes)
- 2 tbsp red pesto
- a handful of basil leaves
- parmesan or pecorino (or vegetarian alternative), to serve

Directions:

1. Boil a large pan of salted water. Add the gnocchi, cook for 2 mins or until it rises to the surface, then drain and tip back into the pan with a splash of reserved cooking water.

2. Add the chargrilled veg, chopped into pieces if large, red pesto and basil leaves. Serve with shavings of Parmesan or pecorino (or vegetarian alternative).

Nutritional Value (Amount per Serving):

Calories: 614; Fat: 18.42; Carb: 108.72; Protein: 16.44

Mediterranean Spelt-Stuffed Peppers

Prep Time: 20 Mins   Cook Time: 25 Mins   Serves: 4

Ingredients:

- 4 large red peppers, halved and deseeded (stems left on)
- 100g fresh sundried tomatoes
- (sometimes called semidried or sun blush), chopped plus 2 tbsp tomato oil

- 1 large red onion, ends trimmed and spiralized on the flat blade of the spiralizer
- 1 large courgette, halved widthways, ends trimmed and spiralized into thin noodles
- 250g pouch pre-cooked spelt
- 100g mixed olives, pips removed and chopped
- 1 small pack of basil, shredded
- green salad, to serve

Directions:

1. Heat oven to 395°F/356°F fan/gas 6. Place the peppers cut-side up on a roasting tray. Drizzle over 1 tbsp of the sundried tomato oil, season with sea salt and black pepper, then roast for 20–25 mins until the peppers are tender.

2. Meanwhile, heat the remaining oil in a frying pan over a medium heat. Add the spiralized red onion. Cook for 2–3 mins until softened then transfer to a bowl.

3. Add in the remaining ingredients and some seasoning. Once the peppers are cooked, generously fill them with the spelt mix and return to the oven for 5 mins to heat through. Serve with a green salad.

Nutritional Value (Amount per Serving):

Calories: 409; Fat: 30.19; Carb: 21.83; Protein: 13.53

Crispy Grilled Feta with Saucy Butter Beans

Prep Time: 2 Mins   Cook Time: 18 Mins   Serves: 4

Ingredients:

- 500ml passata
- 2 x 400g cans butter beans, drained and rinsed
- 2 garlic cloves, crushed
- 1 tsp dried oregano, plus a pinch
- 200g spinach
- 2 roasted red peppers, sliced
- ½ lemon, zested and juiced
- 100g block of feta, cut into chunks
- ½ tsp olive oil
- 4 small pittas

Directions:

1. Put a large ovenproof frying pan over a medium-high heat, and tip in the passata, butter beans, garlic, oregano, spinach and peppers. Stir together and cook for 6-8 mins until the sauce is bubbling and the spinach has wilted. Season, then add the lemon juice.

2. Heat the grill to high. Scatter the feta over the sauce, so it's still exposed,

drizzle with the olive oil and sprinkle over the lemon zest plus a pinch of oregano, then grind over some black pepper. Grill for 5-8 mins until the feta is golden and crisp at the edges.

3. Meanwhile, toast the pittas under the grill or in the toaster, then serve with the beans and feta.

Nutritional Value (Amount per Serving):

Calories: 82; Fat: 4.19; Carb: 5.82; Protein: 6.77

Roasted Cauli-Broc Bowl with Tahini Hummus

Prep Time: 10 Mins   Cook Time: 30 Mins   Serves: 2

Ingredients:

- 400g pack cauliflower & broccoli florets
- 2 tbsp olive oil
- 250g ready-to-eat quinoa
- 2 cooked beetroots, sliced
- large handful baby spinach
- 10 walnuts, toasted and chopped
- 2 tbsp tahini
- 3 tbsp hummus
- 1 lemon, 1/2 juiced, 1/2 cut into wedges

Directions:

1. The night before, heat oven to 395°F/356°F fan/gas 6. Put the cauliflower and broccoli in a large roasting tin with the oil and a sprinkle of flaky sea salt. Roast for 25-30 mins until browned and cooked. Leave to cool completely.

2. Build each bowl by putting half the quinoa in each. Lay the slices of beetroot on top, followed by the spinach, cauliflower, broccoli and walnuts. Combine the tahini, hummus, lemon juice and 1 tbsp water in a small pot. Before eating, coat in the dressing. Serve with the lemon wedges.

Nutritional Value (Amount per Serving):

Calories: 1784; Fat: 118.27; Carb: 157.6; Protein: 44.45

Grilled Vegetables with Cannellini Beans & Vegan Pesto

Prep Time: 15 Mins   Cook Time: 30 Mins   Serves: 4

Ingredients:

- 1 large aubergine, sliced lengthways into ½cm slices
- 2 courgettes, sliced lengthways into ½cm slices
- 250g cherry tomatoes
- 400g can cannellini beans
- crusty bread, to serve

For The Pesto:
- 60g basil leaves
- 20g parsley leaves
- 1 small garlic clove
- 1 lemon, zested and juiced
- 30g pine nuts, lightly toasted, plus 1 tbsp to serve
- 2 tsp nutritional yeast
- 3-4 tbsp olive oil

Directions:

1. Light the barbecue. For the pesto, blitz the basil, parsley, garlic, lemon zest and juice, 30g pine nuts and nutritional yeast together in a food processor. Mix in the olive oil to loosen and season to taste.

2. When the coals are ashen, place the aubergine and courgette slices on the grill. Cook for 2-3 mins, then turn and cook for 2-3 more mins until the veg is softened and slightly shrunken. Add the tomatoes to the grill and cook, turning often until the skins have split and the tomatoes soften. Immediately remove from the grill along with the other veg.

3. Drain the cannellini beans, reserving the liquid from the can, and tip the beans onto a serving platter. Add 2 tbsp of pesto and mix, loosening the bean mixture with some of their reserved liquid.

4. Add the aubergine and courgette slices to the platter and mix gently until lightly coated in the pesto. Scatter the tomatoes on top, then drizzle with more pesto (you can loosen this with more of the reserved bean liquid, if needed). Sprinkle with the extra 1 tbsp pine nuts and serve with crusty bread.

Nutritional Value (Amount per Serving):

Calories: 179; Fat: 8.64; Carb: 19.95; Protein: 7.41

Roasted Summer Vegetables

Prep Time: 10 Mins   Cook Time: 40 Mins   Serves: 4

Ingredients:

- 3 tbsp olive oil
- 1 aubergine, cut into chunks
- 2 mixed coloured peppers, such as orange and red, cut into chunks
- 1 red onion, cut into wedges
- 2 courgettes, cut into chunks
- 4 garlic cloves, smashed

- 3 sprigs of thyme
- 200g cherry tomatoes
- handful of basil leaves
- zest of 1 lemon
- 50g feta, crumbled

Directions:

1. Heat the oven to 395°F/356°F Fan/gas 6. Mix the oil with the aubergine, peppers, red onion, courgette, garlic and thyme in a bowl with sea salt and black pepper. Tip into a large roasting tin, then roast for 30 mins. Add the tomatoes to the pan and return to the oven for 10 mins.

2. Squeeze the garlic from their skins, remove the thyme, then scatter over the basil, lemon zest and crumbled feta.

Nutritional Value (Amount per Serving):

Calories: 827; Fat: 52.71; Carb: 17.61; Protein: 72.99

Roasted Fresh Green Beans

Prep Time: 5 Mins   Cook Time: 10 Mins   Serves: 4

Ingredients:

- 1 pound green beans, trimmed
- 1 tablespoon extra-virgin olive oil

Directions:

1. Preheat oven to 500 degrees F.

2. Spread beans on a large rimmed baking sheet or in a pan large enough to hold them in a single layer. Drizzle with oil; toss to coat well.

3. Roast the beans, turning once halfway through cooking, until tender, about 10 minutes.

Nutritional Value (Amount per Serving):

Calories: 38; Fat: 2.02; Carb: 4.9; Protein: 1.28

Piled-High Vegetable Pitas

Prep Time: 15 Mins   Cook Time: 10 Mins   Serves: 4

Ingredients:

- 1 tablespoon olive oil
- 1 cup canned no-salt-added chickpeas (garbanzo beans),
- rinsed and patted dry
- ½ teaspoon paprika
- ¼ teaspoon garlic powder

- ¼ teaspoon ground cumin
- ⅛ teaspoon ground pepper
- 2 cups Roasted Butternut Squash & Root Vegetables (see Associated Recipes)
- 1 1/3 cups Lemon-Roasted Mixed Vegetables (see Associated Recipes)
- 1 cup fresh baby spinach
- ½ cup cherry tomatoes, halved
- ¼ cup crumbled reduced-fat feta cheese (1 oz.)
- 2 (6 to 7 inch) whole-wheat pita bread rounds, halved horizontally and lightly toasted (see Tip)
- ½ cup hummus
- Lemon wedges

Directions:

1. Heat oil in a 10-inch skillet over medium heat. Add chickpeas; sprinkle with paprika, garlic powder, cumin, and pepper. Cook, stirring frequently, until the chickpeas are lightly browned, 6 to 8 minutes.

2. Transfer the chickpeas to a medium bowl. Add Roasted Butternut Squash & Root Vegetables, Lemon-Roasted Mixed Vegetables, spinach, tomatoes, and feta; toss gently to combine. Serve with pita, hummus, and lemon wedges.

Nutritional Value (Amount per Serving):

Calories: 209; Fat: 8.39; Carb: 28.91; Protein: 6.58

Roasted Butternut Squash & Root Vegetables

Prep Time: 10 Mins   Cook Time: 30 Mins   Serves: 4

Ingredients:

- 3 cups butternut squash, peeled, seeded, and cut into 1-inch pieces
- 1 cup sliced parsnips
- ½ cup sliced carrot
- ½ cup chopped onion
- 1 tablespoon olive oil
- ¼ teaspoon salt
- ⅛ teaspoon ground pepper
- ⅛ teaspoon cayenne pepper

Directions:

1. Preheat oven to 400 degrees F. Combine squash, parsnips, carrot, and onion in a 15-by-10-inch baking pan.

2. Drizzle the vegetables with oil and sprinkle with salt, pepper, and cayenne; toss to coat.

3. Roast, covered, for 20 minutes. Stir the vegetables and then roast, uncovered, until tender and starting to brown, about 10 minutes more.

Lemon-Roasted Mixed Vegetables

Prep Time: 10 Mins   Cook Time: 25 Mins   Serves: 5

Ingredients:

- 1 ½ cups cauliflower florets
- 1 ½ cups broccoli florets
- 2 cloves garlic, thinly sliced
- 1 tablespoon olive oil
- 1 teaspoon dried oregano, crushed
- ¼ teaspoon salt
- ¾ cup diced red bell pepper (1-inch)
- ¾ cup diced zucchini (1-inch)
- 2 teaspoons lemon zest

Directions:

1. Preheat oven to 425 degrees F.

2. Combine cauliflower, broccoli, and garlic in a 15-by-10-inch baking pan. Drizzle with oil and sprinkle with oregano and salt; stir to coat. Roast for 10 minutes.

3. Add bell pepper and zucchini to the vegetables in the pan; stir to combine. Roast until the vegetables are crisp-tender and lightly browned, 10 to 15 minutes more.

4. Sprinkle lemon zest over the vegetables; stir and serve.

Nutritional Value (Amount per Serving):

Calories: 40; Fat: 2.89; Carb: 3.3; Protein: 1.28

Chapter 5: Snacks

Yogurt & Honey Fruit Cups

Prep Time: 10 Mins   Cook Time: 10 Mins   Serves: 6

Ingredients:

- 4-1/2 cups cut-up fresh fruit (pears, apples, bananas, grapes, etc.)
- 3/4 cup mandarin orange, vanilla or lemon yogurt
- 1 tablespoon honey
- 1/2 teaspoon grated orange zest
- 1/4 teaspoon almond extract

Directions:

1. Divide fruit among 6 individual serving bowls. Combine the yogurt, honey, orange zest and extract; spoon over the fruit.

Nutritional Value (Amount per Serving):

Calories: 207; Fat: 0.42; Carb: 51.11; Protein: 0.63

Lemon Garlic Hummus

Prep Time: 10 Mins   Cook Time: 10 Mins   Serves: 1

Ingredients:

- 2 (15.5-ounce) cans garbanzo beans (chick peas), drained with 1/3 cup liquid reserved
- 3 garlic cloves, chopped
- 1/4 cup fresh lemon juice (2 to 3 lemons)
- 3 tablespoons olive oil
- 1 teaspoon salt
- 1 teaspoon ground cumin

Directions:

1. Combine all ingredients in a food processor. Process until mixture is smooth and creamy, and no lumps remain, scraping down sides of bowl as needed.

2. Serve immediately, or cover and chill until ready to serve.

Nutritional Value (Amount per Serving):

Calories: 490; Fat: 41.37; Carb: 27.19; Protein: 6.42

Fresh Is Best Hummus

Prep Time: 5 Mins   Cook Time: 10 Mins   Serves: 1

Ingredients:

- 1 (15-ounce) can garbanzo beans, drained, liquid reserved
- 2 teaspoons minced garlic
- 2 tablespoons fresh lemon juice
- 2 tablespoons olive oil

Directions:

1. In a blender or food processor, process all ingredients except reserved liquid, about 30 seconds. Add reserved liquid until desired consistency.

Nutritional Value (Amount per Serving):

Calories: 604; Fat: 33.38; Carb: 62.05; Protein: 18.34

Homemade Hummus

Prep Time: 10 Mins   Cook Time: 5 Mins   Serves: 1

Ingredients:

- 1 (15.5-ounce) can chickpeas, drained and rinsed
- 1/2 cup nonfat plain yogurt
- 3 teaspoons lemon juice
- 1/2 teaspoon garlic powder
- 1/2 teaspoon onion powder
- 1/4 teaspoon sesame oil
- 1 teaspoon chopped fresh parsley

Directions:

1. In a food processor, combine chickpeas, yogurt, lemon juice, garlic powder, onion powder, and sesame oil. Process until smooth.

2. Spoon into a serving bowl and stir in parsley. Cover and refrigerate until ready to serve.

Nutritional Value (Amount per Serving):

Calories: 424; Fat: 7.78; Carb: 64.39; Protein: 27.04

Nutty White Bean Hummus

Prep Time: 10 Mins   Cook Time: 10 Mins   Serves: 1

Ingredients:

- 2 tablespoons pine nuts
- 1 cup canned cannellini beans, drained, with liquid reserved
- 1 teaspoon grated lemon zest
- 1/4 teaspoon garlic powder
- 1 tablespoon lemon juice
- 1/4 teaspoon salt

Directions:

1. In a skillet over low heat, toast pine nuts until light brown and fragrant.

2. In a medium bowl, mash cannellini beans.

3. Add lemon zest and lemon juice to beans, mixing well. Add garlic powder and salt, and mix thoroughly. Stir in small amounts of reserved bean liquid until desired consistency. Sprinkle with pine nuts and serve.

Nutritional Value (Amount per Serving):

Calories: 39; Fat: 0.88; Carb: 7.86; Protein: 1.76

Greek Salad Cracker Snack

Prep Time: 5 Mins   Cook Time: 10 Mins   Serves: 1

Ingredients:

- 1 cup chopped tomatoes
- 1/4 cup chopped red onion
- 1 cup fresh spinach, coarsely chopped
- 1/3 cup fat-free crumbled feta cheese
- 1/2 teaspoon dried oregano
- 1/4 teaspoon black pepper
- 1 tablespoon canola oil
- 6 multi-grain crispbreads, split in half (we used Wasa)

Directions:

1. In a medium bowl, combine tomatoes, onion, spinach, feta cheese, oregano, pepper, and oil; toss until evenly coated.

2. Top each cracker with an equal amount of tomato mixture and serve.

Nutritional Value (Amount per Serving):

Calories: 685; Fat: 22.04; Carb: 85.25; Protein: 38.85

Greek Isle Mushroom Stuffers

Prep Time: 10 Mins   Cook Time: 10 Mins   Serves: 1

Ingredients:

- 12 large fresh white mushrooms, stems removed and chopped into small pieces
- 1/2 cup finely chopped onion
- 1/4 cup chopped ripe olives
- 2 tablespoons crumbled feta cheese

Directions:

1. Preheat oven to 425 degrees F. Line a baking sheet with aluminum foil. Coat mushroom caps with cooking spray and arrange on baking sheet.

2. Bake 5 minutes. Drain on paper towels, then return to baking sheet; set aside.

3. Coat a medium nonstick skillet with cooking spray. Cook and stir mushroom stems and onion over medium heat, until tender.

4. In a medium bowl, mix mushroom stems, onion, olives, and cheese, then fill mushroom caps with mixture.

5. Bake 5 minutes, or until hot and bubbly. Serve immediately.

Nutritional Value (Amount per Serving):

Calories: 914; Fat: 68.42; Carb: 28.74; Protein: 52.07

7-Layer Mediterranean Dip

Prep Time: 10 Mins   Cook Time: 10 Mins   Serves: 1

Ingredients:

- 1/2 cup nonfat Greek yogurt
- 3 cloves garlic, minced
- 1/8 teaspoon salt
- 1 (10-ounce) container classic hummus
- 1 tomato, diced
- 1/2 cup diced cucumber
- 1 (7.5-ounce) jar marinated artichoke hearts, drained and chopped
- 1/2 cup chopped roasted red pepper
- 1/4 cup crumbled feta cheese
- 2 tablespoons chopped parsley
- Chopped Kalamata olives for garnish
- Olive oil for drizzling

Directions:

1. In a small bowl, combine yogurt, garlic, and salt; set aside.

2. Spread hummus over a 10-inch round serving plate. Layer with tomatoes and cucumber. Dollop yogurt mixture and gently spread.

3. Top with artichoke hearts, red peppers, feta cheese, and parsley. Sprinkle olives and drizzle with olive oil.

Nutritional Value (Amount per Serving):

Calories: 837; Fat: 44.45; Carb: 82.58; Protein: 32.29

Mediterranean Roasted Pepper Dip

Prep Time: 5 Mins   Cook Time: 15 Mins   Serves: 1

Ingredients:

- 1 (7-ounce) jar roasted red peppers, drained and patted dry
- 1 (15-ounce) can chickpeas, rinsed and drained
- 1 (16-ounce) non-fat Greek yogurt
- 2 tablespoons chopped fresh basil
- 1 garlic clove
- 1/8 teaspoon black pepper

Directions:

1. Place all the ingredients in a blender jar and process until thoroughly blended. Serve immediately, or store in the refrigerator in an airtight container until ready to use.

Nutritional Value (Amount per Serving):

Calories: 449; Fat: 8.63; Carb: 73.69; Protein: 22.81

Chapter 6: Salads

Caprese Salad

Prep Time: 10 Mins   Cook Time: 10 Mins   Serves: 4

Ingredients:

- 3 medium tomatoes (3/4 pound total), cut into 8 slices
- 2 (1-ounce) slices part-skim mozzarella cheese, each cut into strips (24 strips total)
- 1/8 teaspoon salt
- Pinch black pepper
- 2 teaspoons extra-virgin olive oil
- 1/4 cup thinly sliced fresh basil leaves

Directions:

1. Arrange tomatoes and cheese alternately on plate, overlapping slightly. Sprinkle with salt and pepper and drizzle with oil. Scatter basil on top.

Nutritional Value (Amount per Serving):

Calories: 59; Fat: 4.21; Carb: 1.2; Protein: 4.18

Mediterranean Fig & Mozzarella Salad

Prep Time: 15 Mins   Cook Time: 5 Mins   Serves: 4-6

Ingredients:

- 200g fine green bean, trimmed
- 6 small figs, quartered
- 1 shallot, thinly sliced
- x ball mozzarella, drained and ripped into chunks
- 50g hazelnut, toasted and chopped
- small handful basil leaves, torn
- 3 tbsp balsamic vinegar
- 1 tbsp fig jam or relish
- 3 tbsp extra-virgin olive oil

Directions:

1. In a large saucepan of salted water, blanch the beans for 2-3 mins. Drain, rinse in cold water, then drain on kitchen paper. Arrange on a platter. Top with the figs, shallots, mozzarella, hazelnuts and basil.

2. In a small bowl or jam jar with fitted lid, add the vinegar, fig jam, olive oil and some seasoning. Shake well and pour over salad just before serving.

Nutritional Value (Amount per Serving):

Calories: 165; Fat: 8.3; Carb: 20.11; Protein: 3.72

Mediterranean Feta Salad with Pomegranate Dressing

Prep Time: 10 Mins   Cook Time: 30 Mins   Serves: 8

Ingredients:

- 2 red peppers
- 3 medium aubergines, cut into chunks, or 15 small, halved
- 6 tbsp extra-virgin olive oil
- tsp cinnamon
- 200g green bean, blanched (use frozen if you can)
- 1 small red onion, sliced into half moons
- 200g feta cheese, drained and crumbled
- seeds 1 pomegranate
- handful parsley, roughly chopped

For The Dressing

- 1 small garlic clove, crushed
- 1 tbsp lemon juice
- 2 tbsp pomegranate molasses
- 5 tbsp extra-virgin olive oil

Directions:

1. Heat oven to 392°F/fan 356°F/gas 6. Heat the grill to its highest setting. Cut the peppers into quarters, then place them, skin-side up, on a baking sheet. Grill until blackened. Place in a plastic bag, seal, then leave for 5 mins. When cool enough to handle, scrape skins off, discard, then set the peppers aside.

2. Place the aubergines on a baking tray, drizzle with olive oil and cinnamon, then season with salt and pepper. Roast until golden and softened – about 25 mins.

3. Meanwhile, combine all the dressing ingredients and mix well. To serve, place the aubergines, green beans, onion and peppers on a large serving plate. Scatter with the feta and pomegranate seeds. Pour the dressing over, then finish with the parsley.

Nutritional Value (Amount per Serving):

Calories: 475; Fat: 30.32; Carb: 12.45; Protein: 39.84

Mediterranean Cobb Salad

Prep Time: 1 Hr   Cook Time: 5 Mins   Serves: 10

Ingredients:

- 1 package (6 ounces) falafel mix
- 1/2 cup sour cream or plain yogurt
- 1/4 cup chopped seeded peeled cucumber
- 1/4 cup 2% milk

- 1 teaspoon minced fresh parsley
- 1/4 teaspoon salt
- 4 cups torn romaine
- 4 cups fresh baby spinach
- 3 hard-boiled large eggs, chopped
- 2 medium tomatoes, seeded and finely chopped
- 1 medium ripe avocado, peeled
- and finely chopped
- 3/4 cup crumbled feta cheese
- 8 bacon strips, cooked and crumbled
- 1/2 cup pitted Greek olives, finely chopped

Directions:

1. Prepare and cook falafel according to package directions. When cool enough to handle, crumble or coarsely chop falafel.

2. In a small bowl, mix sour cream, cucumber, milk, parsley and salt. In a large bowl, combine romaine and spinach; transfer to a platter. Arrange crumbled falafel and remaining ingredients over greens. Drizzle with dressing.

Nutritional Value (Amount per Serving):

Calories: 175; Fat: 13.26; Carb: 6.58; Protein: 8.6

Garden Pasta Salad

Prep Time: 15 Mins   Cook Time: 15 Mins   Serves: 8

Ingredients:

- 6 cups (about 12 ounces) cooked penne pasta
- 2 cups shredded cooked boneless skinless chicken breasts
- 3/4 cup chopped red onion
- 3/4 cup chopped red or green bell pepper
- 3/4 cup sliced zucchini
- 1 can (4 ounces) sliced black olives, drained
- 1 teaspoon red pepper flakes
- 1 teaspoon salt (optional)
- 1 can (10 3/4 ounces) condensed reduced-fat reduced-sodium cream of chicken soup, undiluted
- 1/2 cup lemon juice
- 1/2 cup grated Parmesan cheese
- 1/2 cup chopped fresh basil (optional)
- 1/4 cup chopped fresh parsley (optional)

Directions:

1. Combine pasta, chicken, onion, bell pepper, zucchini, olives, red pepper flakes and salt in large bowl; toss lightly.

2. Combine soup and lemon juice in small bowl; mix well. Pour soup mixture

over pasta salad; mix well.

3.Sprinkle with Parmesan cheese, basil, and parsley.

Nutritional Value (Amount per Serving):

Calories: 260; Fat: 4.56; Carb: 36.31; Protein: 18.87

Tangy Steamed Green Bean Salad

Prep Time: 10 Mins   Cook Time: 7 Mins   Serves: 4

Ingredients:

- 1 pound fresh whole green beans, washed, ends trimmed off
- 2 tablespoons extra-virgin olive oil
- 2 tablespoons red wine vinegar
- 1 tablespoon Dijon-style mustard
- 1 tablespoon water
- 1/4 teaspoon garlic powder
- 1/4 teaspoon black pepper
- 4 green onions, finely chopped
- 10 cherry tomatoes, cut in half

Directions:

1.Steam green beans in a steamer (or use a steaming basket in saucepan) for about 5 minutes until bright green and still slightly crisp. Immediately rinse under cold running water, until cool to the touch. Drain. Place in a serving dish. In a small bowl, combine olive oil, red wine vinegar, mustard, water, and garlic powder with a small whisk or spoon. Pour over green beans. Add green onions and tomatoes, toss well, and serve.

Nutritional Value (Amount per Serving):

Calories: 349; Fat: 25.13; Carb: 7.86; Protein: 22.02

Greek Isles Salad

Prep Time: 5 Mins   Cook Time: 10 Mins   Serves: 1

Ingredients:

- 2 large tomatoes, cut into wedges
- 1/3 cup red onion slivers
- 8 large pitted black olives
- 2 tablespoons Feta Vinaigrette (See Note: To make your own Feta Vinaigrette, in a small bowl, whisk together 2 tablespoons olive oil, 3 tablespoons red wine vinegar, 1 teaspoon dried basil, and 2 tablespoons crumbled feta cheese. Makes about 1/3 cup.)

Directions:

1. Arrange tomatoes, red onion, and black olives on 4 salad plates, distributing evenly. Drizzle with dressing.

Nutritional Value (Amount per Serving):

Calories: 127; Fat: 4.53; Carb: 19.99; Protein: 3.93

Marinated Steak Salad

Prep Time: 5 Mins   Cook Time: 15 Mins   Serves: 1

Ingredients:

- 2 tablespoons olive oil
- 1 tablespoon fresh lime juice
- 1 small onion, minced
- 1 tablespoon crushed red pepper
- 1/4 teaspoon salt
- 1 (1-pound) beef flank steak
- 1 head romaine lettuce, cut into
- bite-sized pieces
- 6 plum tomatoes, sliced into wedges
- 2 tablespoons sliced olives
- 1/4 cup (1 ounce) crumbled reduced-fat feta cheese

Directions:

1. In a large resealable plastic bag, combine the oil, lime juice, onion, crushed red pepper, and salt; mix well. Add the steak then seal, and turn to coat. Marinate in the refrigerator for at least 4 hours, turning occasionally.

2. Drain the steak, discarding the marinade.

3. Coat a medium skillet with nonstick cooking spray. Heat the skillet over high heat, add the steak, and cook for 4 to 5 minutes per side for medium-rare, or to desired doneness. Slice the steak thinly across the grain.

4. Place the lettuce on a serving platter and arrange the steak slices and tomato wedges over it. Sprinkle with olives and feta cheese. Serve immediately.

5. To make this a gluten-free recipe, use seasonings with no added starch from a gluten-containing source, and nonstick cooking spray with no flour added.

Nutritional Value (Amount per Serving):

Calories: 960; Fat: 44.32; Carb: 96.94; Protein: 52.84

Mediterranean Pear Salad

Prep Time: 5 Mins   Cook Time: 10 Mins   Serves: 1

Ingredients:

- 4 cups mixed baby greens
- 2 Anjou pears with peel, cored, and cut into chunks
- 2 tablespoons crumbled feta cheese
- 2 tablespoons fat-free balsamic vinaigrette

Directions:

1.Arrange greens in 4 salad bowls; evenly distribute pears and feta on top. Drizzle with dressing.

Nutritional Value (Amount per Serving):

Calories: 1321; Fat: 69.67; Carb: 104.09; Protein: 76.02

Almost Greek Salad

Prep Time: 5 Mins   Cook Time: 10 Mins   Serves: 1

Ingredients:

- 2 large tomatoes, cut into wedges
- 1/3 cup red onion slivers
- 2 large pitted black olives, sliced
- 2 tablespoons Feta Cheese Dressing

Directions:

1.Combine tomatoes, red onions and olives in salad bowl and toss with dressing.

Nutritional Value (Amount per Serving):

Calories: 236; Fat: 17.04; Carb: 19.69; Protein: 4.11

Mediterranean Shrimp Salad

Prep Time: 5 Mins   Cook Time: 10 Mins   Serves: 1

Ingredients:

- 12 cooked jumbo shrimps, thawed
- 1/2 red onion, thinly sliced
- 1 (15-ounce) can chickpeas, no
- salt-added, rinsed and drained
- 4 tablespoons balsamic vinegar
- 2 tablespoons olive oil

- 2 tablespoons fresh basil, slivered
- 1 head romaine lettuce, chopped

Directions:

1. In a medium bowl, combine shrimps, red onion, Balsamic vinegar, oil, and basil; mix well. Cover and chill 2 hours, or until well chilled.

2. Evenly divide lettuce among 4 plates. Top with shrimp mixture and garnish with tomato wedges. Serve immediately.

Nutritional Value (Amount per Serving):

Calories: 921; Fat: 49.5; Carb: 96.05; Protein: 3.07

It's Greek To Me Dressing

Prep Time: 5 Mins   Cook Time: 10 Mins   Serves: 2

Ingredients:

- 2 tablespoons canola oil
- 3 tablespoons red wine vinegar
- 1 tablespoon fresh basil or 1
- teaspoon dried basil
- 2 tablespoons crumbled feta cheese

Directions:

1. In a shaker bottle with a lid, combine all ingredients. Shake well to blend.

Nutritional Value (Amount per Serving):

Calories: 524; Fat: 45.93; Carb: 6.23; Protein: 21.37

Chickpea and Aubergine Warm Salad

Prep Time: 10 Mins   Cook Time: 20 Mins   Serves: 4

Ingredients:

- 1 large aubergine (eggplant), cut into 2cm cubes
- 1 garlic clove, skin on and bashed with the back of a knife
- 4 tablespoons of extra-virgin olive oil
- 1 teaspoon of paprika
- 1 tin of chickpeas, well drained
- salt and pepper for seasoning
- parsley leaves and nasturtium to scatter on top

Directions:

1. Heat up the oil in a large, non-stick frying pan, add the garlic and cook in the oil to infuse its scent into it for 1 minute. Add the aubergine, stir well

until well coated with the oil, then turn the heat to medium-low, cover with a lid and allow the hot oil and the steam to cook the vegetables gently for 15 minutes. Stir from time to time.

2. When the aubergines look soft and slightly caramelized, add the chickpeas and paprika, stir well and cook, uncovered, over medium heat for 4-5 minutes. Taste for salt and adjust accordingly.

3. Serve warm topped with parsley and nasturtium leaves and a grounding of black pepper.

Nutritional Value (Amount per Serving):

Calories: 160; Fat: 8.01; Carb: 18.03; Protein: 5.52

Roasted Veggie & Quinoa Salad

Prep Time: 5 Mins   Cook Time: 5 Mins   Serves: 1

Ingredients:
- 2 cups mixed salad greens
- 1 cup roasted root vegetables (see associated recipes)
- ½ cup cooked quinoa (see associated recipes)
- 1-2 tablespoons vinaigrette (see associated recipes)
- 1 tablespoon crumbled feta cheese
- 1 tablespoon sunflower seeds

Directions:

1. Combine greens, roasted vegetables and quinoa; drizzle with vinaigrette. Top the salad with feta and sunflower seeds.

Nutritional Value (Amount per Serving):

Calories: 2793; Fat: 253.67; Carb: 82.93; Protein: 46.5

Summer Shrimp Salad

Prep Time: 5 Mins   Cook Time: 5 Mins   Serves: 1

Ingredients:
- 1 ¼ pounds raw shrimp (21-25 count), peeled and deveined
- ¼ cup extra-virgin olive oil
- 10 sprigs fresh thyme
- 4 cloves garlic, crushed
- ¼ teaspoon salt
- ¼ teaspoon ground pepper
- ¼ cup lemon juice
- 1 medium English cucumber, diced

- 3 large heirloom tomatoes, chopped
- ½ cup chopped fresh basil, plus more for garnish

Directions:

1. Preheat oven to 350 degrees F.

2. Toss shrimp with oil, thyme and garlic on a rimmed baking sheet. Sprinkle with salt and pepper. Bake until the shrimp are pink and firm, 8 to 10 minutes.

3. Transfer the shrimp to a large bowl (discard thyme and garlic). Add lemon juice and stir to coat. Gently stir in cucumber, tomatoes and basil. Arrange the shrimp and vegetables in a serving bowl. Serve drizzled with any dressing left in the bowl and garnish with more basil, if desired.

Nutritional Value (Amount per Serving):

Calories: 331; Fat: 9.77; Carb: 32.46; Protein: 36.23

Tuna & Olive Spinach Salad

Prep Time: 10 Mins   Cook Time: 10 Mins   Serves: 1

Ingredients:

- 1 ½ tablespoons tahini
- 1 ½ tablespoons lemon juice
- 1 ½ tablespoons water
- 1 5-ounce can chunk light tuna in water, drained
- 4 Kalamata olives, pitted and chopped
- 2 tablespoons feta cheese
- 2 tablespoons parsley
- 2 cups baby spinach
- 1 medium orange, peeled or sliced

Directions:

1. Whisk tahini, lemon juice and water together in a bowl. Add tuna, olives, feta and parsley; stir to combine. Serve the tuna salad over 2 cups spinach, with the orange on the side.

Nutritional Value (Amount per Serving):

Calories: 397; Fat: 22.73; Carb: 14.09; Protein: 38.55

Cucumber, Tomato & Avocado Salad

Prep Time: 10 Mins   Cook Time: 10 Mins   Serves:

Ingredients:

- 2 tablespoons extra-virgin olive oil
- 1 tablespoon sherry vinegar
- 1 teaspoon orange zest
- ½ teaspoon salt
- ½ teaspoon honey
- ½ teaspoon ancho chile powder
- 1 large English cucumber, chopped
- 1 cup cherry tomatoes, halved
- 1 ripe avocado, halved, pitted and chopped

Directions:

1. Whisk oil, vinegar, orange zest, salt, honey and chile powder in a large bowl. Add cucumber; toss gently. Cover and let marinate for 15 minutes. Fold in tomatoes. Gently fold in avocado. Serve immediately.

Nutritional Value (Amount per Serving):

Calories: 122; Fat: 10.49; Carb: 7.1; Protein: 1.49

Warm Exotic Fruit Salad

Prep Time: 15 Mins   Cook Time: 5 Mins   Serves: 4

Ingredients:

- 2 cardamom pods, crushed
- 1 tbsp fresh mint, chopped
- 1 piece preserved stem ginger from a jar, finely chopped, plus 2 tbsp of the syrup
- 1 pineapple, prepared and cut into chunks (prepared weight 500g)
- 1 papaya, peeled seeded and cut into chunks
- 1 kiwi fruit, sliced

Directions:

1. Place the cardamom pods, mint, ginger syrup and 2 tbsp water into a pan. Bring to the boil.

2. Remove from the heat and cool for 15 minutes.

3. Pour over the prepared fruit, stand for 10 minutes and serve.

Nutritional Value (Amount per Serving):

Calories: 200; Fat: 4.61; Carb: 30.65; Protein: 10.85

Green Salad with Edamame & Beets

Prep Time: 15 Mins   Cook Time: 15 Mins   Serves: 1

Ingredients:

- 2 cups mixed salad greens
- 1 cup shelled edamame, thawed
- ½ medium raw beet, peeled and shredded (about 1/2 cup)
- 2 tablespoons red-wine vinegar
- 1 tablespoon chopped fresh cilantro
- 1 tablespoon extra-virgin olive oil
- ⅛ teaspoon salt
- Freshly ground pepper to taste

Directions:

1. Arrange greens, edamame and beet on a large plate. Whisk vinegar, cilantro, oil, salt and pepper in a small bowl. Drizzle one tablespoon of the dressing over the greens and toss gently to coat. Drizzle the remaining dressing over the entire salad.

Nutritional Value (Amount per Serving):

Calories: 1324; Fat: 92.14; Carb: 21.65; Protein: 98.59

Traditional Greek Salad

Prep Time: 15 Mins   Cook Time: 5 Mins   Serves: 4

Ingredients:

- 3 tablespoons extra-virgin olive oil
- 1 tablespoon lemon juice
- 1 tablespoon red-wine vinegar
- 1 teaspoon dried oregano
- ¼ teaspoon salt
- ¼ teaspoon ground pepper
- 2 ripe medium tomatoes, cut into 3/4-inch dice
- 1 ½ cups diced cucumber (3/4-inch)
- 1 cup diced green bell pepper (3/4-inch)
- ⅓ cup thinly sliced red onion
- ¼ cup quartered pitted Kalamata olives
- ½ cup diced feta cheese (2 1/2 ounces)

Directions:

1. Whisk oil, lemon juice, vinegar, oregano, salt and pepper together in a large bowl. Add tomatoes, cucumber, bell pepper, onion, olives and feta. Toss to coat.

Nutritional Value (Amount per Serving):

Calories: 138; Fat: 10.88; Carb: 6.43; Protein: 4.66

Chapter 7: Desserts

Vanilla Almond Fruit Dip

Prep Time: 10 Mins   Cook Time: 15 Mins   Serves: 10

Ingredients:

- 2 1/2 cups fat-free half-and-half
- 1 package (4-serving size) fat-free sugar-free vanilla instant pudding mix (dry)
- 1 tablespoon sugar substitute
- 1 teaspoon vanilla extract
- 1 teaspoon almond extract
- Fresh fruit (optional)

Directions:

1. Beat half-and-half, pudding mix, sugar substitute, vanilla, and almond extracts in mixing bowl with electric mixer at medium speed for 2 minutes. Serve immediately or refrigerate until ready to serve. Serve with fruit for dipping, if desired.

Nutritional Value (Amount per Serving):

Calories: 64; Fat: 0.89; Carb: 12.18; Protein: 1.83

Blood Orange Olive Oil Cake

Prep Time: 10 Mins   Cook Time: 20 Mins   Serves: 8

Ingredients:

- Cooking spray or extra-virgin olive oil
- 1 medium blood orange
- 1 1/4 cups all-purpose flour
- 1/2 cup medium-grind cornmeal
- 2 teaspoons baking powder
- 1/4 teaspoon baking soda
- 1/4 teaspoon fine salt
- 2/3 cup plus 2 tablespoons granulated sugar, divided
- 1/2 cup whole-milk plain yogurt
- 3 large eggs
- 1/2 cup extra-virgin olive oil
- 4 paper-thin half moon-shaped blood orange slices (optional)

Directions:

1. Arrange a rack in the middle of the oven and heat to 350°F. Grease a 9- by 5-inch loaf pan with cooking spray or oil; set aside.

2. Using a vegetable peeler, remove the zest from the orange. Cut the zest into thin strips and set aside. Juice the orange and set aside 1/4 cup (save the remaining juice for another use).

3. Whisk the flour, cornmeal, baking powder, baking soda, and salt together in a medium bowl; set aside.

4. Whisk 2/3 cup of the sugar and the 1/4 cup blood orange juice together in large bowl. One at a time, whisk in the yogurt, eggs, and olive oil. Whisk the flour mixture into the wet ingredients, giving the mixture 20 good turns with the whisk until just combined. Fold in the zest strips.

5. Transfer the batter into the prepared pan. Top with the blood orange slices and remaining 2 tablespoons sugar. Bake until the top is springy and golden-brown, and a wooden skewer inserted in the center comes out with just a few crumbs attached, 50 to 60 minutes.

6. Let the cake cool in the pan on a wire rack for 20 minutes. Carefully unmold the cake, flip it back to be right-side up, and return to the rack to cool completely.

Nutritional Value (Amount per Serving):

Calories: 247; Fat: 10.08; Carb: 34.63; Protein: 4.43

Balsamic Berries with Honey Yogurt

Prep Time: 10 Mins   Cook Time: 20 Mins   Serves: 8

Ingredients:

- 8 ounces strawberries, hulled and halved, or quartered if very large (about 1 1/2 cups)
- 1 cup blueberries
- 1 cup raspberries
- 1 tablespoon balsamic vinegar
- 2/3 cup whole-milk plain Greek yogurt
- 2 teaspoons honey

Directions:

1. Toss the strawberries, blueberries, and raspberries with the balsamic vinegar in a large bowl. Let sit for 10 minutes. Stir the yogurt and honey together in a small bowl. Divide the berries among serving bowls or glasses, and top each with a dollop of honey yogurt.

Nutritional Value (Amount per Serving):

Calories: 172; Fat: 1.79; Carb: 38.92; Protein: 2.78

BrûlÉEd Ricotta

Prep Time: 5 Mins   Cook Time: 5-10 Mins   Serves: 4

Ingredients:

- 2 cups (16 ounces) high-quality whole-milk ricotta cheese
- 1 teaspoon finely grated fresh lemon zest (from 1 lemon)
- 2 tablespoons honey
- 2 tablespoons granulated sugar
- Fresh raspberries, for serving (optional)

Directions:

1. Place the ricotta, lemon zest, and honey in a large bowl and stir to combine. Divide among 4 (6-ounce) ramekins, and place the ramekins on a rimmed baking sheet. Evenly sprinkle the tops with the sugar.

2. Arrange an oven rack in the highest position. Place the baking sheet on the rack and turn on the broiler. Broil until the ricotta is golden-brown and bubbling, 5 to 10 minutes. Alternatively, you can use a kitchen torch to brown the tops of the ricotta. Let cool for 10 minutes. Top with raspberries, if using, and serve.

Nutritional Value (Amount per Serving):

Calories: 322; Fat: 16.18; Carb: 31.45; Protein: 14.53

One-Bowl Yogurt and Honey Olive Oil Cake

Prep Time: 10 Mins   Cook Time: 1 Hr   Serves: 8-12

Ingredients:

- 1 cup whole or 2% plain Greek yogurt
- 2/3 cup olive oil, plus more for coating the pan
- 2/3 cup honey
- 1 tablespoon finely chopped fresh thyme leaves
- 1 teaspoon finely grated lemon zest
- 3 large eggs
- 1 1/2 cups all-purpose flour
- 1/2 teaspoon baking powder
- 1/2 teaspoon baking soda
- 1/4 teaspoon salt

Directions:

1. Arrange a rack in the middle of the oven and heat to 325°F.

2. Grease a 9-inch round cake pan or springform pan lightly with oil. Line the bottom with parchment paper, and grease the paper if using a cake pan.

3. Whisk together the yogurt, olive oil, honey, thyme, and lemon zest in a large bowl. Add the eggs, one at a time, whisking well after each addition. Add the flour, baking powder, baking soda, and salt. Stir with a rubber spatula until the batter is almost smooth, with just a few small lumps, but do not overmix.

4. Transfer the batter to the cake pan, and use a spatula to spread it out evenly. Bake until the top is lightly browned and a tester comes out clean, 40 to 45 minutes.

5. Transfer the cake to a cooling rack and let it cool for 10 minutes before removing it from the pan. Run a knife around the pan to loosen. If using a springform pan, unclasp the sides. Otherwise, flip the cake onto a plate and flip it back onto the rack or serving plate. Serve warm or at room temperature.

Nutritional Value (Amount per Serving):

Calories: 297; Fat: 16.81; Carb: 34.56; Protein: 3.68

Domenica Marchetti's Carrot Polenta Cake with Marsala

Prep Time: 10 Mins   Cook Time: 40 Mins   Serves: 6-8

Ingredients:

- 1/2 cup extra-virgin or light olive oil, plus more for the pan
- 1 cup granulated sugar
- 2 large eggs
- 1/2 cup dry Marsala wine
- Finely grated zest of 1 lemon
- Finely grated zest of 1 orange
- 1 1/4 cups all-purpose flour
- 1/2 cup finely ground polenta
- 2 teaspoons baking powder
- 3/4 teaspoon fine sea salt
- Pinch of freshly grated nutmeg
- 2 cups shredded carrots (about 3 large)
- Powdered sugar for dusting

Directions:

1. Heat the oven to 375°F/gas 5. Lightly coat an 8-in/20-cm square or round baking pan with olive oil and set aside.

2. In a large bowl, whisk together the olive oil, granulated sugar, eggs, Marsala, and the lemon and orange zests until well blended (the sugar will not completely dissolve).

3. In a separate medium bowl, whisk together the flour, polenta, baking powder, salt, and nutmeg. Pour the flour mixture into the egg mixture, whisking all the while to avoid lumps. Using a silicone spatula or wooden spoon, stir in the shredded carrots. Scrape the batter into the prepared baking pan.

4. Bake for 35 minutes, or until a cake tester inserted into the middle of the cake comes out clean. Transfer the pan to a rack to cool for 20 to 30

minutes. Remove the cake from the pan and set it on the rack to cool to room temperature.

5. Transfer the cake to a decorative platter. Dust the cake lightly with confectioners' sugar right before serving.

Nutritional Value (Amount per Serving):

Calories: 331; Fat: 18.17; Carb: 37.9; Protein: 5.16

Whipped Yogurt with Apples and Walnuts

Prep Time: 10 Mins   Cook Time: 40 Mins   Serves: 4

Ingredients:

- 1 cup plain Greek yogurt
- 1/2 cup heavy cream
- 1 tablespoon honey
- 2 tablespoons unsalted butter
- 2 firm apples, cored and chopped
  into small 1/2-inch cubes
- 2 tablespoons sugar
- 1/8 teaspoon ground cinnamon
- 1/4 cup walnut halves, toasted
  and coarsely chopped

Directions:

1. Combine the yogurt, cream, and honey in a bowl, and beat vigorously with a hand mixer until the mixture thickens and forms soft peaks. (You can also use a stand mixer, or whip by hand using a whisk.)

2. Warm the butter in a large skillet over medium heat. Add the apples and 1 tablespoon sugar to the pan. Stir well and cook the apples for 6 to 8 minutes, stirring occasionally to avoid sticking, until they just begin to soften. Once softened, sprinkle the apples with the remaining sugar and the cinnamon, and cook for an additional 2 to 3 minutes. Remove from the heat and let sit for 5 minutes to cool slightly.

3. To serve, spoon a generous serving of whipped yogurt into each bowl, and top with warm apples and toasted walnuts.

Nutritional Value (Amount per Serving):

Calories: 215; Fat: 12.96; Carb: 21.3; Protein: 5.84

Hazelnut & Olive Oil Shortbread

Prep Time: 10 Mins   Cook Time: 50 Mins   Serves: 18-24

Ingredients:

- 1 1/4 cups hazelnut meal
- 3/4 cup flour
- 1/4 cup brown sugar
- 1/4 cup powdered sugar, plus 1/4 cup for glaze
- 1 teaspoon kosher salt
- 1 lemon, zested and juiced
- 1 teaspoon vanilla
- 1/2 cup extra-virgin light olive oil

Directions:

1. Heat the oven to 375°F. Whisk together the hazelnut meal, flour granulated sugar, 1/4 cup powdered sugar, salt and lemon zest. Whisk in the vanilla and olive oil. The dough will be sandy and quite crumbly.

2. Press the dough firmly into a 8x8-inch (or 9x9-inch) dish. Bake for 20 minutes or until just lightly browned around the edges. Immediately cut the shortbread into diamonds or squares. Let cool completely before lifting them out of the pan, however.

3. Meanwhile, whisk together 1 tablespoon of the lemon juice and the remaining 1/4 cup powdered sugar, and drizzle over the warm cookies.

Nutritional Value (Amount per Serving):

Calories: 107; Fat: 7.5; Carb: 9.13; Protein: 1.78

Blueberry Almond Chia Pudding

Prep Time: 10 Mins   Cook Time: 8 Hrs   Serves: 1

Ingredients:

- ½ cup unsweetened almond milk or other nondairy milk beverage
- 2 tablespoons chia seeds
- 2 teaspoons pure maple syrup
- ⅛ teaspoon almond extract
- ½ cup fresh blueberries, divided
- 1 tablespoon toasted slivered almonds, divided

Directions:

1. Stir together almond milk (or other nondairy milk beverage), chia, maple syrup and almond extract in a small bowl. Cover and refrigerate for at least 8 hours and up to 3 days.

2. When ready to serve, stir the pudding well. Spoon about half the pudding into a serving glass (or bowl) and top with half the blueberries and almonds. Add the rest of the pudding and top with the remaining blueberries and almonds.

Nutritional Value (Amount per Serving):

Calories: 490; Fat: 20.06; Carb: 72.46; Protein: 11.27

Berry-Mint Kefir Smoothies

Prep Time: 5 Mins   Cook Time: 5 Mins   Serves: 2

Ingredients:

- 1 cup low-fat plain kefir (see Tip)
- 1 cup frozen mixed berries
- ¼ cup orange juice
- 1-2 tablespoons fresh mint
- 1 tablespoon honey

Directions:

1.Combine kefir, berries, juice, mint to taste and honey in a blender. Process until smooth. (The smoothies will keep in the refrigerator for up to 1 day or in the freezer for up to 3 months.)

Nutritional Value (Amount per Serving):

Calories: 333; Fat: 7.69; Carb: 57.1; Protein: 9.7

APPENDIX RECIPE INDEX

Made in the USA
Las Vegas, NV
05 January 2025

15896248R00061